Practical Shamanism
A Guide for Walking in Both Worlds
by
Katie Weatherup

A Hands over Heart Publishing Book

PRACTICAL SHAMANISM, A GUIDE FOR WALKING IN BOTH WORLDS

First Edition

First Printing

September 2006

Cover Design by Jennifer Dyer

Editing by William H Stoddard

Book layout and text design by Laura Kate Barrett

ISBN 0-9778154-0-4

Library of Congress Control Number: 2006929550

TABLE OF CONTENTS

For my mother, Cari, who sees me as I truly am—light alike—and loves me unconditionally.

And for my father, John, who loves me enough to read something as alien to his worldview as shamanism, just it.

INTRODUCTION

I'm partial to the quotation, attributed to Woody Allen, "There is no question that there is an unseen world. The problem is how far is it from midtown and how late is it open?" Shamanism holds an answer to that question that has resonated for many people, across many cultures throughout the ages. My understanding of that answer is that the unseen world is right on top of midtown, over, under, and around it, and it's open whenever we care to visit, day or night. This spiritual world doesn't close down on bank holidays and one of the best things about the shamanic version of the unseen world is that it's custom tailored for each seeker.

This book is about my experience of the shamanic world and is intended as a road map to help you find your own. Your shamanic world will undoubtedly look different from mine and likewise very different from that of the indigenous people of the Amazon jungle. Nevertheless, everyone who chooses to explore the shamanic world may find wonder, magic, and healing there.

In addition to a road map for exploring shamanism, I intend this book to provide an array of options for self-healing, using the basic tools of shamanic journeying and a few other relevant techniques. We are energetic and spiritual beings as much as we are physical ones. Every living thing is imbued with energy, recognized by many names across the world, such as 'chi' in China, 'mana' to the Hindu and 'ki' in Japan. When I talk about energy, I am referring to this universal life energy. This is the energy of our spirit, the energy that creates our vitality. This book provides means to support and nurture the energetic aspects of our beings. When those aspects come into alignment, the material world will follow. This book offers information and ideas that you can apply to your normal, everyday life.

In this section, you will find information on the benefits of shamanism and my perspective on it. In Part One, I present background information on shamanism and provide instructions for learning shamanic journeying. Part Two deals with the shamanic worldview, our energetic relationship to the world, and concepts of right relationship. In Part Three, I explore more advanced concepts, such as past life work and shadow work. This is advanced shamanic work that you can begin to explore once you have mastered the basics. In the final section, I share some of my favorite journeys and experiences with shamanism.

Shamanism can sound very mysterious and has often been represented as something for a chosen few, requiring great sacrifice and/or an indigenous lifestyle. While there are some phenomenal shamanic practitioners for whom this is true, this is far from the only way to experience shamanism. Shamanism doesn't demand long trips to the Amazon jungles and it's not restricted to a few blessed individuals. People come to spiritual initiation in a variety of ways, some gentle, some dramatic. The fact that some people have had very dramatic, life-changing first experiences with shamanism does not mean that's the only or even preferred means of having a shamanic connection become part of your life.

Shamanism isn't difficult or mysterious, although it does operate from some premises that are outside mainstream Western thought. It provides a way of understanding some part of the cosmos that we can't see or touch directly. While the notion of interacting with spiritual guides may seem far-fetched in our modern, scientific age, this worldview has arisen independently in indigenous cultures throughout the world. The actual tools and techniques of shamanism are straightforward, relatively simple, and very thoroughly tested.

When I embarked upon my spiritual path, one of my realizations was that I was not going to be able to use other people for my spiritual connection. It was rather dismaying because it seemed that there were so many people who were already so gifted and so far along. I was seeing the unseen world as the faintest hint of a shadow. Meanwhile those around me seemed to be getting it in Technicolor.

I made every effort to persuade those who seemed to see territory so clearly to make the connection for me, giving my power away rather freely. I was blessed to find teachers who gently but firmly steered me toward learning to see for myself, offering road maps for how to get there, but steadfastly refusing to be my link to my spirituality. When I began learning about shamanism and shamanic journeys, I suddenly had a way to have the spiritual connection I yearned for, without giving away my power to human intermediaries.

Shamanism provides a direct and immediate spiritual connection to your own personal spirit guides and angels, the natural world around you, and the divine, however you conceive it to be. Furthermore, you gain access to information about yourself, your life path and choices, and the world around you. It offers a way to ask questions about the mundane aspects of life—food, love, and career—as well as the great questions, such as the meaning of life and your spiritual purpose.

For me, owning my own power and having a direct connection to the spiritual was one of the greatest gifts of shamanism, but there are many others as well. Immense healing resources are available to you through shamanism. Our spirit guides and helpers can remove negative energy and restore life force energy. They can help you walk through your greatest fears in a gentle way. They can even hold you while you cry. Within the shamanic world we can experience divine love, acceptance, and unconditional support. In one of my early journeys, my guide took me to a barren rock in the middle of the ocean and sat there with me until I understood that however alone and isolated I might feel, my guides were always there with me. I was never truly abandoned or forsaken.

Shamanic practices and understanding provide a path to right alignment or right relationship with the world. When you are in right relationship to the world, the universe will work in mysterious and overt ways to advance your goals and well-being. Luck and serendipity become a constant part of your life, allowing you to connect with wonderful people, succeed in your goals and business endeavors, and generally receive gifts that far exceed anything you requested.

Shamanic journeying offers tools for self-mastery and growth. You can use shamanic journeys to access the deepest parts of your being. We all have patterns and ways of walking the world that don't serve us, yet we persist in them again and again. Conscious insight into the whys and wherefores of those patterns isn't always enough to shift them. By accessing the unconscious aspects of yourself through shamanic journeys, you can shift and change those patterns overnight. Many philosophies are based on the idea that with a healthy mastery of self, you don't need to change the external world in order to find peace and happiness. Shamanism is one of the pathways to this mastery.

Whenever you select a teacher or a book or a healer, it's important to understand their "take" on the subject. With shamanism appearing in so many different cultures and times, teachers and practitioners approach the subject in a wide variety of ways. Rather than saying one approach is better than another, I simply want to be clear about the approach I use for teaching shamanism. My approach to shamanism is *not* a traditional one.

I've spent a lot of time studying, exploring, and trying a variety of shamanic practices and ideas. I've woven them together into a fabric of my own making. Because I value this process of creating your own spiritual belief and understanding, I urge you to do the same with my shamanic teachings. Take what serves you and leave the rest. If what I say doesn't fit for you or if your guides tell you something different, go with what feels right to you.

My personal approach to shamanism doesn't include much ritual, even through shamanism is often a very ritualistic practice. For example, many shamanic practitioners begin by honoring the elements or burning herbs. My emphasis is on giving you the tools to connect with your guides, as simply and easily as possible. If ritual is a good match for your practice, your guides will teach you what rituals will serve you best.

This book is designed for someone living in our busy modern world. Our world is far from perfect, but anyone who waxes too nostalgic about the past hasn't paid very close attention to history. I adore e-mail and computers and the wide array of opportunities for experiences that are available. We have more choices and options and access to ideas than our ancestors have ever known. We can create communities that nurture who we are, rather than learning to survive in the communities we are born into. Of course this creates greater complexity and new challenges. It can be harder to find what we want, with so many choices. It can be more difficult to create downtime with so much to do. I hope the shamanic information I provide will help you to stay centered, choosing what nurtures you and feeling whole and fulfilled in our busy world.

My goal in writing this book is not to produce a definitive work on shamanism. I'm not the expert and I'm still learning. Instead, I strive to communicate my experience clearly and give you the ideas and tools needed to begin your own shamanic explorations. Rather than persuading you of my truth, I want you to be able to find your own wisdom and knowledge along your spiritual path.

I have found the spirit world eager to communicate, filled with love, and possessing quite a sense of humor. When I asked for a blessing/permission to beginning teaching shamanism I was shown a huge group of spirits. One stepped forward and offered me a folded piece of paper on a silver tray, formally and officially inviting me to teach. I got the distinct impression that I had been being nudged in this direction for some time, so they were playing with me, saying, "Of course we support you in doing this, but if you need an engraved invitation, we can do that too." So, in turn, allow me to formally invite you, on behalf of your spirit guides, to step into shamanic reality and experience that world first hand.

PART I
BACKGROUND AND INSTRUCTIONS FOR LEARNING
SHAMANIC JOURNEYING

CHAPTER 1 — GENERAL BACKGROUND

Shamanism and methods of shamanic journeying are found throughout the world in diverse cultures. So, it follows that there are many flavors, approaches, and understandings of these same terms. Shamanic journeying provides a direct connection to the spirits who are the real teachers. Even people with the same shamanic tradition will get different information and lessons from their spirit guides.

The flavor of shamanic journey I work with is based loosely on the form developed by Michael Harner in the 1970's. I have, of course, adapted his methods and studied with teachers with completely different backgrounds. Still, I consider Michael Harner's method, which he dubbed "core shamanism," to be my shamanic tradition.

Ordinary and Nonordinary Reality

Core shamanism was developed from Michael Harner's explorations of shamanism in many cultures. He noted that despite vast differences in geographic location and cultural practices, many shamanic practices are the same throughout the world. He took the practices that appeared in all or most cultures and developed an approach to present them to a modern, technological audience.

In this model, the shamanic practitioner learns to shift their awareness at will between our normal everyday world (which is referred to as ordinary reality) and the shamanic world, known as nonordinary or shamanic reality. It's like when two people are talking at the same time and you choose to tune into one and tune the other person out. Most of us learn to tune into ordinary reality all the time. This is completely appropriate for our human existence. It keeps us from walking into walls and allows us to deal directly with the physical world. Most shamanic practitioners still spend the majority of their time with their attention and awareness firmly and primarily focused on the physical world of ordinary reality.

In ordinary reality, we encounter things with physical form and the laws of science and physics apply. In nonordinary reality, we encounter things with energetic form. Myths, dreams, thoughts, intention all contain energy that we can explore and experience in nonordinary reality. Nonordinary reality is a place to perceive the symbolic truth of our existence. Again, both ordinary and nonordinary realities are around us all the time. When we focus on nonordinary reality, the laws of physics still impact our physical bodies, just not our energetic bodies. Even if we never do a shamanic journey, we will still connect to nonordinary reality in dreams and through intuition. With shamanic journeys, we simply choose at any given moment whether to focus the majority of our attention on ordinary or nonordinary reality.

To explore the realm of nonordinary reality, the shamanic practitioner moves into an altered state of consciousness. This allows them to interact with spirits—guides, teachers, power animals, ancestors, spirits of nature, ascended masters, angels and deities, and so forth. Historically, most cultures have relied upon some form of communication with spirits. Traditionally a shaman would journey to interact with the spirits for power, healing, and information, for themselves and for their communities.

Throughout this book, I will talk about spirit guides. By this I mean benevolent beings without physical form who help us, in shamanic reality as well as in our daily lives. They offer information, guidance, wisdom, protection, and healing. Some people choose to understand these spirit guides as aspects of themselves or their higher selves. Others understand their spirit guides in a religious context as angels, saints, or deities.

How we choose to understand our spirit guides and the universe in general is merely the framework we set up in our minds to deal with the vast, unknowable mystery of the universe. One framework isn't more valid or correct than another. So, when I talk about shamanism, I am talking about one way of understanding the unseen world. There are many other equally valid stories, allegories, ideas, and frameworks to conceptualize the unseen world. You don't have to believe in spirit guides or my framework in order to learn shamanic journeying and benefit from it. There are many beliefs in the metaphysical community that I neither accept nor reject, I simply acknowledge.

Shamans through the ages have used a variety of means to induce a shamanic state of awareness, including drugs, dance, and meditation. In traditional shamanic practices from indigenous cultures there are often elements of spiritual machismo and great hardship. Michael Harner talks about his initial experiences of shamanism as including a series of scary, dangerous, and very uncomfortable tests. Often traditional shamans came to their calling through a near death experience. While that kind of shamanic path is available to those who would seek it, I don't recommend it or teach it. It's possible to learn shamanic techniques in a gentle way without ever jumping into a pool of freezing water, taking harsh drugs, or fasting for days. All of these things will induce an altered state and have been used in traditional shamanic cultures, but there is a gentler, more comfortable path available.

Listening to a drum or rattle is one of the safest and easiest approaches. Shamanism is not just about being able to walk in both worlds—our everyday ordinary world and nonordinary reality—it's also about being able to walk in those worlds at will, controlling which reality you perceive and when. That's another reason I don't recommend using drugs. They take away the ability to choose which reality you focus your attention on.

Seeing into both worlds all the time, without any control, is considered delusional. Whether the schizophrenic is seeing things that aren't there or is simply seeing into both worlds uncontrollably, the outcome is the same—the inability to function effectively in the normal, physical world. So that concept of turning your shamanic perceptions on and off at will is vitally important. A sense of self-discipline and solid ego strength are very important for a shamanic practitioner.

I'm often asked what shamanic journeying is like. For me, it has similarities to dreaming, visualization, and watching a movie. It's not passive; if you aren't actively focusing, you'll slip into dozing. But if you're trying to control it, information won't come in. This balance sounds complicated but isn't all that hard with practice. It's just different from what most people have experienced.

A good analogy is that of Tai Chi, an internal martial art form. In Tai Chi, you are actively moving and the postures have martial applications, but you are also soft and relaxed as you move through the form. Being relaxed and receptive as well as active and focused is the ideal state for the shamanic journeying experience. This sounds harder than it is.

When you journey, you begin to see pictures and images and meet with spirit beings. You have the ability to control what you do and say, but not what those around you do or say. As with anything else, people get information in different ways, seeing things, hearing things, feeling things, knowing things to be true, etc. Your spirit guides will pick the most suitable way to communicate with you. I have had students reject perfectly valid and wonderful shamanic experiences because the actual experience was different from what they imagined. So it's important to be open to whatever you experience, rather than judging your experience against strong preconceived notions.

Is shamanic journeying the right tool for you?

Sometimes, when I speak on the subject of shamanism, I worry that I sound like a used car salesman or a religious zealot. My goal isn't to sell or convert, but it's easy for my great passion and enthusiasm for the subject to make it sound like I believe shamanism is the key to all that ails you. While it is an incredibly powerful tool that can be applied in many ways for many problems, it's not a magical fix. Before I talk about how to engage in shamanic journeying, I want to talk about what it will and won't do for you and how to determine if it's the right tool.

If you are seeking a stronger sense of yourself as a spiritual being, shamanism can be very helpful. Shamanism can provide a stronger connection to your intuition, sources of support, and wisdom and tools that allow you to improve your relationship with yourself and the world around you. Shamanism, like so many things, is only helpful for people who are interested in self-empowerment and growth. You must be willing to take an active role in your growth and healing for shamanism to be beneficial.

If you are in crisis, utterly overwhelmed, desperate, or suicidal, learning shamanic journeying isn't the best place to focus your energies. Shamanic journeying takes concentration and effort to learn. It's great for personal growth and a powerful tool, but teaching yourself shamanic journeying is not a good crisis strategy. This is not to say your life must be perfect to learn shamanic journeying—after all, we look for new tools when things aren't working. Just bear in mind that while, in the long term, shamanism may be one of your best sources of help and support, it's a skill that will take time to develop, so it's not the shortest path to help and support.

Likewise, if you are having an overwhelming and negative response to the energetic world around you—seeing scary spirits or feeling energetically attacked—I don't recommend you open those senses further by learning shamanic journeying. Sometimes the services of an experienced holistic healer can be helpful, but more often it's appropriate to seek the services of someone using more conventional forms of treatment. Conventional therapy, medicine, and psychiatric care aren't perfect and don't address everything, but they can give someone the stable foundation they need to benefit from something like shamanism or energy healing.

I'm a great believer both in conventional psychological healing and in metaphysical approaches. If someone is having significant problems in their life, a combination of conventional therapy and nonconventional healing can be the fastest and optimum path to health and wholeness. Sometimes lessons in dealing with others in a healthy way, setting good emotional boundaries, and understanding and releasing destructive patterns are addressed more easily and quickly in therapy than with shamanic journey. I know I wouldn't be as far along in my own quest for health and wholeness without all the pieces—conventional therapy as well as energetic and shamanic healing.

I find that some people have the belief that if they are spiritually healthy and whole, they won't feel darker emotions, like anger, sadness, and jealousy. They seek metaphysical tools to allow them to transcend (i.e., not feel) their emotions. This is not how shamanism works. Like many other healing techniques, shamanism is wonderful for helping people not get stuck in one emotional state, like anger or fear. Not feeling these uncomfortable emotions at all doesn't reflect spiritual health, but a rather severe withdrawal from the experience of being human. Indeed, people can get caught up in the idea that being an evolved person means they never feel certain things, so they shame themselves or suppress natural emotions.

Shamanism will not help you never to be angry or sad. Instead, shamanism may teach you how to embrace and use your anger in a positive and empowering way or nurture yourself when sadness arises. It may also help you not to be angry or sad all the time. But it's important when we visualize health and spiritual wholeness that we include the full human experience, rather than seeking to disown the less comfortable parts.

Shamanic journey offers immediate access to spiritual guidance and to the divine. It's a way to access the love and support and wisdom of beings that are totally on your side. Shamanism offers a way to understand life from a different perspective and learn new approaches for moving through the world. But shamanism is still just one tool and technique for growth and healing. How much energy and attention and introspection you bring to your shamanic practice largely determines what the benefits will be.

Our spirit guides want to help us and support us, but there is little they can do unless we choose to grow and change. Shamanism is not a substitute for human touch and relationships. It's not a substitute for a healthy diet, plenty of rest, and getting regular physical exercise. It won't replace modern medicine. Your guides can help you learn how to live the fullest life possible, but it's important to remember to nurture all aspects of your being—physical, mental, emotional as well as spiritual. Shamanism is just one piece of the puzzle.

Adapting traditional shamanism for our modern time

When learning about shamanism, it's important to pay attention to cultural context as you develop your own practice. The needs, demands, and challenges that gave rise to a certain spiritual practice may not exist in another culture. Michael Harner looked at elements in many shamanic cultures and then created an appropriate shamanic framework for a modern technological audience. It was his knowledge of the needs of his own culture as much as his study of indigenous cultures that allowed him to develop a shamanic approach that has resonated for hundreds of thousands of people.

It's valuable and fascinating to study indigenous forms of shamanism. It's fine to incorporate practices from other cultures that you find beautiful and useful into your own spiritual practice. However, it's unwise to take a spiritual practice from another culture and assume that you understand the meaning without thoroughly studying that culture.

For those of us living in the modern, technological world, it's essential to embrace the fact that we live in this world, with a different set of gifts and challenges than someone living one thousand years ago in the African rain forest. In our society, for the most part, we worry about making time for our next meal, not whether there will be food available. We learn in classrooms in a day or a week and from books, rather than through years of apprenticeship.

Many people in the spiritual community seem to have the idea that a practice is higher in some spiritual hierarchy because it came from a Native American or from Tibet. I disagree with the implied notion that one people or one culture is wiser or better than another. Every culture has gifts and strengths and challenges. Every race has its cruel and willfully ignorant members as well as beautiful and loving people.

The spiritual leaders I've found worth listening to say very much the same thing, whether of European, Tibetan, Native American, or African decent. I love it when someone can offer me a glimpse of the world from a different vantage point, but that doesn't innately give them a greater monopoly on universal truth. The wisdom they have to offer depends entirely on what they've done with their experience.

So don't let anyone tell you they are having a better or more meaningful shamanic experience because they spent thousands of dollars to travel to Peru and learn from traditional shamans under the influence of hallucinatory drugs, while you read a book or attended a class and learned to journey to a drumbeat. There are people who like to jump out of perfectly good airplanes because they love the rush, but I prefer to minimize the adrenaline experience. The person who loves big, dramatic, challenging kinds of experiences will pick a different spiritual path than I have and find other books to read.

My use of the term "shaman" is a good example of the difference between a modern culture context and an indigenous culture context. I use the term "shamanic practitioner" to describe what I do and encourage my students to do the same. I choose to reserve the term "shaman" for the people occupying that role in indigenous societies because the role is unique. The indigenous shaman was entrusted by the people of the community to act as their spiritual intermediary. I teach shamanism to reduce the need for spiritual intermediaries.

When you embark on a shamanic path it's important not to give up your power, not to your guides, not to your human teachers. Every suggestion, whether you receive it in shamanic reality or ordinary reality, must be run through your discernment. You, and you alone, must decide whether the suggestion fits for you. This is not the traditional style of teaching where shamanism is concerned.

In traditional shamanic training, the student did what they were told by their guides and human teachers—even if it was scary or dangerous—as proof of their commitment to walking that path. While walking through fear and stretching yourself can be very powerful, I don't believe there's any need for the process of learning shamanic journeying to be such an endeavor. The spirit guides and human teachers are our guides and advisors, but we are the ones who are responsible for living our lives and the consequences of our choices.

Looking at a traditional culture, it's easy to see how a difficult initiation process could be useful. The fact that the shaman had gone through difficult trials that the people of the community had not faced helped to establish that they were different and special. It gave them more authority and prestige in keeping with their role as a spiritual intermediary and healer. Having someone you perceive as powerful and knowledgeable tell you that you will get better has a huge psychological impact, all on its own. Also, among a group of people struggling to meet their survival needs, it was unrealistic for everyone to pursue shamanic training. Having tests and challenges was a good way to make sure the prospective shaman was deeply committed. Finally, shamanic training was conducted on a one-on-one basis, not in classrooms or through a book, so the teacher could effectively gauge for each student how far to push them without doing physical or psychological damage.

While I can see and acknowledge the effectiveness of having a few gurus (i.e., shamans) within a tribe of traditional people for some of the reasons I discussed above, I don't think it's a good fit within our modern culture. Our culture teaches us to trust other people—experts outside ourselves—rather than to listen to our own internal knowledge and wisdom. Shamanism isn't for a select few blessed and gifted souls; it's available for anyone who feels called to explore it and is willing to put some time into learning. This process will help you learn to trust yourself and find the path that's right for you, rather than the one other people tell you is correct. I teach people to be their own experts as shamanic practitioners and follow a path that's gentle and safe and non-threatening.

CHAPTER 2 — LEARNING SHAMANIC JOURNEYING

Perhaps the most important thing I can tell you as you begin learning shamanic journeying is that if you are going to try it at all, take the time and effort to give it an honest try. Some people get great results on their first try. Most people, myself included, have a few frustrating attempts before they really get the hang of it. Be patient with yourself and the technique. Once you get it, you'll have it forever.

The shamanic world

Shamanic or nonordinary reality can be understood to include three distinct places: Lower World, Upper World, and Middle World. These three worlds are believed to be connected by a tree with roots that extend into Lower World and branches that reach into Upper World. The trunk of the tree links all three worlds.

Lower world is thought to be below us and is the archetypal nature realm. This world contains much vital energy. In Lower World, we meet power animals—spirit guides in animal form. This world is associated with the physical aspects of our existence, such as our life energy. The Lower World holds energies that help our physical, human form to thrive and grow, while keeping it protected. It is a safe, beautiful, and wonderful place.

Sadly, Christian ideologies put hell below, which can cause some confusion and apprehension for those raised with that religious background. Lower World has absolutely no connection to Christian hell, nor to the after-death underworld that appears in some non-Christian myths. It's kind of funny to imagine the confusion as the

Christian missionaries attempted to communicate the horrors of their hell below them to indigenous people, for whom Lower World, also below them, is a place of blessings and power.

Upper world is another safe and beautiful place. In this case, the Christian idea of heaven, although different, was not so diametrically opposed to many indigenous views of Upper World. Upper World is the realm of ascended masters and teachers and is found above us. It tends to be more ethereal and less solid than Lower World, although everyone experiences these places differently. In Upper World, you can dance among the stars and connect with guides that help nurture your spiritual aspects. Did you ever want to ask Jesus Christ or Buddha what he really meant when he said this or that? They can be found in Upper World, as can Quan Yin, Kali, Pele, Grandmother Spider, the archangel Michael, and so on.

Middle World includes the shamanic aspects of our normal, physical reality. Middle World isn't good or bad, but it is complex. If you've ever walked into a place that felt wonderful, stepping into shamanic reality in this location would be even more intensely positive. On the other hand, those places that make your skin crawl in the waking world are best to avoid in shamanic reality unless you're going there to do specific work.

Within Middle World, you can see the energetic representations of all things—energetic cords, symbolic representations of relationships, the movement of energy. The human dreamtime is found in Middle World. It is also the place where you may run into disincarnate spirits or souls waiting to move on. They may have chosen to linger or they may have gotten lost or stuck. These being are not spirit guides and should not be viewed in the same way.

Within Middle World is your sacred garden, your personal place of power. For some people, the foundation of their garden is the nonordinary or shamanic aspect of a real, physical place that they connected with at one time or another. Mine is in a specific location in the American Southwest. Hank Wesselman's is in Hawaii. For others, their sacred garden is a place they've never been, but simply know to be their heart's home.

Often people already have a garden of some kind set up from previous guided meditations or other exercises. One of the great things about your garden is that you get to create and explore and change it to suit you. You are not constrained by logic— a mountain stream can divide the desert and the forest as it runs into the ocean. If you step behind the waterfall, you can enter a crystal cave. In most places in shamanic reality, if you don't like the landscape, you need to move yourself; you can't change the scenery. Within your garden, you can create whatever landscape you wish. Often your garden grows and expands each time you explore it. Within your garden you are completely safe and protected. You have absolute power over who enters this space. Your garden is your personal space in shamanic reality, where you can go to rest, heal, learn, grow, and explore.

In his book, Journey to the Sacred Garden, Hank Wesselman talks about how, by shifting aspects of your garden, you can shift your own internal landscape dramatically. What you find in your garden is symbolic and a mirror of your own soul or self. This is a good option for people who are uncomfortable with the idea of communicating with spirit guides. I have had the experience of going to my garden when I was feeling particularly unhappy with the world and finding the sky black and overcast with a huge thunderstorm. When that happens, I let the storm run its course and wait for the sky to clear. I invariably come back from my journey tired but centered and at peace with the universe again. Everything isn't perfect, but my sense of right relationship to the universe has been restored.

Getting where you're going in shamanic reality

By now it should be clear that shamanic reality is a huge, diverse place with more to explore than anyone could ever travel through in a lifetime. So, amid all this vastness, it's important to be able to get where you want to go. You accomplish this with focus and intention. When you first begin a journey, you will set your intent for where you want to go and what you want to accomplish. Here are some examples of intentions:

- I will journey to Lower World and meet my power animal.

- I will journey to Upper World and ask my teacher what are the next steps on my spiritual path.

- I will journey to my sacred garden and ask for a healing related to my issues around anger. I ask that the appropriate guides meet me in my garden.

- I will journey to my garden and ask my guides for help in healing the mother–daughter relationships in my ancestral line. I ask that the appropriate guides meet me in my garden.

- I will journey to Lower World to find a power animal for Amanda.

An example of a poorly worded intention would be "I'm going to journey in shamanic reality to find out what the next steps are on my spiritual path". This isn't a good intention because shamanic reality is huge and it doesn't express a clear idea of where you're going or how this information will be obtained.

Before you begin a journey, have a clear and precise intent for what you want to accomplish, where you will go first, and who you will meet. Stay focused on that intention until you have accomplished the initial goal. So if your intent was "I will journey to Lower World and meet my power animal," you'll keep saying that intent over to yourself until you arrive in Lower World and meet your power animal.

Once you have arrived at your selected destination, met with the spirit guides you intended, and asked for whatever you wanted, your focus shifts. Then you need to focus on being present and receptive to what they have to tell you or show you. Staying present and receptive may sound hard, but with practice it isn't. It's like when you're talking to someone. It's easy to tell when someone is totally focused on what you are saying and really listening. On the other hand, there are times when someone is talking and our attention wanders to what we will say next or another subject entirely. Be a good listener when you're asking your guides for help.

If listening isn't a strong point for you, ask for your guides help in learning that skill. You can also apply some basic meditation techniques. If stray thoughts intrude, acknowledge and release them without struggling to make them go away. Simply bring your attention back to the journey every time you find that it has wandered. In general, because shamanic journeying is so interactive, it is much easier than meditation, which requires you to clear and quiet the mind.

Sometimes your spirit guides will have something that is really important for you to see or hear. Even through your intent is very clear and you're focusing on it, they may give you some information that they feel you should know. Since the spirits are our teachers and our guides, information that they go out of their way to volunteer is worth paying attention to. But, the vast majority of the time, if we state a clear intent and stay focused on it, it will allow us to accomplish exactly what we intend.

The paths to Lower World, Upper World, and our sacred gardens

Whenever I begin a journey, I start by going to Lower World, Upper World, or, most often, my garden. From there, my guides will often take me other places to accomplish the goal of my journey. But these three places are the ones I go to on my own.

Regardless of where I am going, I always start out visualizing myself in a real place in nature. From that place, I then visualize myself taking a path or route to my destination. When you select your place in nature to begin your journey it can be anywhere, as long as it's real or was real at one time—the property you grew up on as a child, for example. It's important not to pick a place in nature that is in your sacred garden because that's one of the places you're traveling to.

To get to Lower World, you will need to find a way to go down. There are many options for what path you choose. You can use a hole in the ground, caves, a well, a whirlpool, the inside of a volcano, a ladder, or stone stairs. Going down through the roots of a tree and then through underground passages is the approach I use. As you go down, remember that you're not confined to your physical body in the same way, so you can squeeze through tiny cracks and openings. Keep moving along your path until you get the sense of dropping out into Lower World.

If you're going to Upper World, start at your place in nature and then find a way to go up. You can climb a tree, swirl up with smoke, simply fly up, climb a mountain or a ladder or a stairway, use a Mary Poppins-type umbrella, take a hot air balloon, or go up a rope. Again, ordinary reality physics don't apply, so you can fly up. As you move into Upper World, you may get the slight sensation of pushing through a barrier, like a bubble or membrane, as you arrive in Upper World. One thing I've found with Upper World is that there seem to be levels. Sometimes you can move past that membrane and look around and there's no one there, even though you had set your intent clearly to meet a guide.

When that happens, just keep going up through another membrane and another, until you get to up to where your guide is.

When going to your sacred garden, you'll also start at a real place in nature. In this case, you're staying in Middle World, so you won't go up or down. Instead, find or create a path that takes you to your garden. Personally, I go into a tree and go out an along a path just a little underground until I pop out in my garden. You could also walk along a path to get to your garden, take a train, ride a bike, swim, etc.

Regardless of where you are, when you hear the drum call back or if you decide to return before the call back, come back along the same path that you started with. Come up from Lower World, down from Upper World, or across from your garden and back to the place in nature that you started off visualizing yourself at. Your return along this path will likely happen much faster and in less detail than your initial outgoing trip.

This is because during your outgoing trip, you were spending time sinking fully into an altered state of consciousness. Coming back, that's not needed, so you can zip right along the return path. Spend a little while hanging out in this place in nature and then bring your attention fully back to being in your body. Give yourself a moment and then wiggle your toes and fingers and open your eyes. The journey is complete.

This process of starting at a real place in nature, then traveling to your destination, and returning in the same manner may seem elaborate, but there are good reasons for it. When you start by visualizing yourself in a real place in nature and then go to your destination, you make the transition into an altered state of awareness and shamanic reality slowly and gradually, which makes it easier. While it may take you a journey or two to select the path that is easiest for you to follow, once you choose that path, always use the same one. If you go up to Upper World in smoke, always go up in smoke. If you go to Lower World down a whirlpool, always use that whirlpool.

While you will initially pick times when you are calm and centered to do shamanic journeying, ultimately this is a tool that you will want to be able to use when you're tired and stressed and emotional and generally out of synch with the world. By going through these steps, the experience of every successful journey you've ever taken will be on your side and you will be able to shift smoothly into a journey state, no matter how keyed up you were when you started

In addition, by taking the time to go and come back through the same steps, you clearly shift your awareness into shamanic reality and then shift it back to ordinary reality at the end. I initially learned shamanic journeying without using this process. Since I could simply drop straight into shamanic reality, I didn't see the point of the place in nature. But when I tried this method, I found that it allowed me to return my awareness to ordinary reality with virtually no spaceyness or disorientation. Simply going straight in and straight out, without the place in nature, left me feeling like I'd just woken up from a long afternoon nap—dazed and not completely awake. So I highly recommend taking the extra minute or two in every journey to use these steps.

However, if you are in the middle of a shamanic journey and something brings your awareness back to ordinary reality, you can pick up your journey where you left off, rather than starting over. Simply visualize yourself back in the place in shamanic reality where you last were and continue with your journey. For example, if you were talking about the nature of karma with a spirit guide when a sound outside startled you, you could simply shift your awareness back to that discussion with your guide.

Our spirit guides

There are many different flavors and types of spirit guides. They may appear as animals or in human form. They may be fairies, elementals, or deities. The most common guides we work with are power animals and teachers, which I will discuss in more detail. While our power animals deal more with protection, support, and power, our teachers help us primarily with wisdom, perceiving things clearly, and getting information. Both power animals and teachers help with healing. Of course, there's no hard and fast rule and each guide will show up at the perfect time to help you with a specific endeavor. As I learn new skills, I often have new guides show up. For example, when I did my training on helping souls cross over, a new teacher came in to work with me.

Throughout this book, I will use the term spirit guide to refer to any helping spirit that has chosen to come into relationship with you. It could be a power animal, an archangel, or your great-great-grandmother. All new spirit guides should be met in Lower World, Upper World, or in your sacred garden. Unless you are meeting the nature spirits or guardians of a specific place, do not accept spirit guides that you meet in Middle World outside your sacred garden.

Power animals

Power animals are spirit guides in animal form. When they aren't helping their person, power animals are found in Lower World. Even if someone never journeys in shamanic reality, they still have one or more power animals. It is believed that when a child is born, a benevolent spirit in animal form looks at the infant and sees how helpless they are. That spirit takes pity on the child and becomes their ally and protector. Often a person's power animal will be an animal that they have a strong affinity for. When someone collects bear or horse figures, it's a good bet that that animal is their power animal.

In ordinary reality, a power animal is a source of protection and power. It's your power animal's job to make sure that the idiot driving way too fast doesn't hit you and that if a rock falls out of the sky it lands next to you, not on you. They work on our behalf to keep the physical world safe and positive for us. A loss or lack of a power animal can result in everything from listlessness to being accident prone to chronic illnesses. A strong connection to a power animal provides a source of energy and support and enhances the flow of your own energy.

If you do shamanic journeying, additional power animals will come to you. In addition to their other functions, I look to my power animals to feel safe in shamanic reality, wherever my travels take me. They guide me to where I need to go, show me what I need to know, and generally help and support me in any journey I select. For complicated endeavors, such as soul retrieval, my power animals will team up with my spiritual teachers and they will work together to guide and assist me.

Sometimes people do a shamanic journey and find that the power animal that is waiting for them is not the one they expect. Someone who has always felt a deep, profound connection to bears, for instance, might be concerned if that animal didn't show up as a power animal. That doesn't mean that this person doesn't have a bear for a power animal; they almost certainly do. However, it may mean that the bear will continue to provide the protection and guidance in their life in ordinary reality but a different animal will work with them in shamanic reality. It can also mean a new animal is choosing to come into relationship with them. The more work we do with shamanic reality, the more power animals will come to assist us.

For power animals, it's important to accept whatever power animal chooses to come into a relationship with you, even if it isn't one of the classic power animals (for example, a squirrel or a mouse rather than a bear, golden eagle, wolf, or mountain lion). If an unexpected animal comes forward, it has some specific gifts for you. Sometimes an animal will show up that you aren't comfortable with. When that happens, the animal is offering to help you with some important lesson, often embracing aspects of yourself that you have disowned or rejected.

For example, one woman had a crocodile show up as a power animal, which she found scary until she realized what a powerful protector this animal was. At the time, she was struggling with holding boundaries and standing up for herself and a crocodile was the perfect ally in that situation.

Sometimes an animal may seem scary at first, but will make a point of showing its softer side, like a wolf rolling on its back or a mountain lion letting you feel how soft its fur is or licking your face. While I have occasionally told guides in human form that I didn't feel comfortable working with them and asked for a different guide, I have never done that with a power animal who came forward. If you get a power animal that's uncomfortable, you aren't obligated to work with them, but there are reasons for that animal being there, so it's good to give it an honest try.

Oddly enough, I've found my students more likely to reject the animal that they expect or want. So if you get a classic, popular power animal such as a wolf or golden eagle, it doesn't mean you're making it up. When I did my first journey to find a power animal, the animal that showed up was one of the classic ones and I started to tell myself (and it) that I was just making this up. My animal conveyed through her body language that I was hurting her feelings by rejecting her. I apologized profusely and we've worked closely together ever since.

Everything is symbolic in shamanic reality and the spirits are prepared to show themselves to us using whatever symbols resonate best for us. They want to communicate with us and are more flexible than we are. So, if there are a disproportionate number of bears that show up as power animals, that is all to the good for both sides. Some people end up working with one power animal; other people, like me, work with a menagerie.

Teachers

In Upper World you can meet with a spiritual teacher. Our teachers are spirit guides who usually appear to us in human form, as opposed to animal form. They provide wisdom, healing, and information. They show us things we need to see and teach us how to do things. They provide guidance along our spiritual path.

Our teachers may just look like ordinary people or they may be well-known deities. One classmate of mine had Pele for a spiritual teacher. The archangel Michael shows up sometimes for me. When dealing with a deity, religious figure, or archetype, you are getting the flavor or aspect of that being that is best suited to you. It's important to remember if Buddha shows up for you in flip flops and a baseball cap, that's not *the* Buddha, it's an aspect of him and someone else will have a different, but equally valid experience. Most often, though, people get teachers they can't identify specifically as this figure or that archetype.

When teachers give you information about a question, the first thing they do or say is the most important aspect of the answer. If I do a journey to ask about what I could do to eat more healthfully, my teacher might show me an experience in a past life of not having enough to eat that needs to be healed. She might then show me piles of vegetables, followed by showing me eating on a regular schedule. The past life healing is the most important for me to address if I want to eat more healthfully.

Preparation for shamanic journeying

When journeying, it is important to ensure, as much as possible, that you won't be interrupted. Be sure to turn the phone off and pick a time when you're unlikely to be disturbed. It is abrupt and unpleasant to be startled out of a journey state and can leave you feeling spacey and off-center. If you ever are startled out of a journey, spend a few minutes focusing on the intent that your awareness, attention, and life force come back fully present to ordinary reality. I like to use a drumming tape or CD with headphones when I journey, because it cuts down on ambient noise and distractions.

To journey by the method I will describe, you'll need a CD or tape with some kind of drumming, rattling, or percussive instrumentation that is specifically designed for shamanic journeying. It needs to have a monotonous beat of 4-5 beats per second and a call back at the end. Or you can get a friend to play a drum or rattle for you. If someone is playing for you, ask that they keep a monotonous beat of 4-5 beats per second and play for 15 minutes, at the end of which they should give you a prearranged call back consisting of four much slower beats, then very rapid beats, then four slow beats, then very rapid beats.

It's important always to come back when the call back happens. If you need more time, you can take another journey by resetting the drumming, but it's important to be disciplined about going in and out at will. Of course, if you feel done before the call back happens, you can always come back early, but it's nice to just hang out in shamanic reality. It's a good place to get recharged and there's always the opportunity to just spend time with your guides, which strengthens the relationship. For all of us who excel at doing and struggle with just being, learning to be in shamanic reality without having to do anything can be both challenging and rewarding. But always come back when the drum call back sounds.

Drumming CDs and tapes are readily available. Look for a tape or CD that is specifically for shamanic journeying. For ease, I will refer to drumming henceforth, but there are numerous instruments that can be used for shamanic journeying. I don't recommend drumming for yourself while you're journeying: not that that isn't a good experience, but for your first few journeys you'll likely need all your concentration. Traditional shamans often have an assistant who takes over drumming for them while they journey.

When you're first learning to journey, it's good to pick a time when you feel calm and centered, but not sleepy. With practice it will become easier and you'll be able to journey easily even when you're sleepy or stressed. But, initially, pick a time when you're in a good space to have this experience.

I generally choose to lie down when I journey. It's more comfortable and then I don't have to pay attention to not falling over. However, if you have a tendency to fall asleep when you journey or are especially tired, sitting up in a comfortable position can help you stay awake. It's good to make sure you're physically comfortable, not too cold or hot, and in a comfortable position. You don't want the needs of your body distracting you while you're journeying.

Before you begin your journey, set your overall intent. If you are feeling at all apprehensive, you can say a little prayer or simply voice your request that your guides and helping spirits assist you in being completely safe and protected. I find that this kind of request helps people put aside whatever anxiety they may have about doing a shamanic journey. A sample affirmation would be, "I will be completely safe and protected during the shamanic journey I am about to take. I will move into an altered state easily and perceive clearly and accurately what my guide show me."

If you have any issues after your first journey attempts, such as not remembering your journey, not being able to get where you are going, feeling anxious, or getting confused information, use an affirmation before you start to tell yourself that you will have a good experience. Always state your affirmation in the positive; for example, "I will remember my journey" instead of "I won't forget what happens."

Journey to Lower World

A good first shamanic journey is a journey to Lower World. In this journey you will go down to Lower World, look around and hang out, and then return when you hear the drum call back.

Intention: I will journey to Lower World.

To begin your journey, get comfortable and start the drumming. In your mind, state any affirmations you wish to use to set your overall intent for the experience. Your affirmation only needs to be stated once. Give yourself a minute or two to adjust to the drums and relax. Think about your intention and say it over to yourself. Until you arrive at your destination, keep focusing on that intent by repeating it to yourself: I will journey to Lower World.

Begin your journey by deliberately using your imagination. Imagine yourself in a real place in nature and find a way to go down. There are infinite possibilities including going down the roots of a tree, a whirlpool, a cavern, a well, caves, a staircase, an elevator. Eventually you should get the feeling of landing, arriving, or popping out into Lower World. If one way doesn't work, try a different path.

You may need to experiment with several paths before you find one that works. Also, keep moving and don't stop until you reach Lower World, even if it means going back and trying another path. At some point, there will be a subtle shift from imagining to perceiving. You may or may not feel this transition, but if you trust that it's happening and keep practicing, eventually you will feel when that shift occurs.

When you arrive in Lower World, spend some time looking around. It may be day or night. You may find yourself in a desert, in a forest, in the mountains, at the ocean, or somewhere else. You may meet animals (mythical or real) or nature spirits. When you hear the drum call back, return using the same route up to your spot in nature. The ascent will likely be much faster than the descent. Then, bring your awareness to your body and the place you are sitting or lying.

Give yourself a moment to focus on being fully present in ordinary reality before you open your eyes or move. Then, if you choose, write down your experiences.

Journey to meet your power animal

In this next journey, you will journey to Lower World to meet your power animal. Include in your intent that your power animal will be waiting when you arrive. When you meet your power animal, it may want to share information or it may tell you about how it will work with you. If your power animal offers information, that's great, but don't go with a separate question because, starting out, the simpler your journey intent, the easier it will be to stay focused on it.

- Start the drumming.

- Set your overall journey intent or affirmation if you choose.

- Set your intention for the journey:

  I will journey to Lower World to meet my power animal. I ask that my power animal be waiting for me when I arrive in Lower World.

- Imagine yourself in your place in nature that you used previously to go down.

- Go down to Lower World.

- Experience the journey.

- Return using the same path you went down when the drum call back sounds. First go into the place in nature and then bring your awareness back to your body.

Journey to Upper World

The journey to Upper World is very similar to the journey to Lower World, except that you find a way to go up instead of down.

- Start the drumming.

- Set your overall journey intent or affirmation if you choose.

- Set your intention for the journey:

  I will journey to Upper World.

- Imagine yourself in your place in nature and find a way to go up.

- Keep going up until you find yourself in Upper World.

- Look around and explore.

- Return using the same path you went up when the drum call back sounds. First go into the place in nature and then bring your awareness back to your body.

Journey to meet your teacher

After you have explored Upper World on your own, you will want to meet your teacher. Again, this is a spirit guide who appears in human form. As with your journey to meet your power animal, don't go with questions the first time, but if your teacher offers information, that's fine.

- Start the drumming.

- Set your overall journey intent or affirmation if you choose.

- Set your intention for the journey:

  I will journey to Upper World to meet my teacher. I ask that my teacher be waiting for me when I arrive.

- Imagine yourself in your place in nature and go up the same way you did before.

- Keep going up until you find yourself in Upper World and see someone waiting for you.

- Meet with your teacher and get to know them.

- Return using the same path you went up when the drum call back sounds. First go into the place in nature and then bring your awareness back to your body.

Journey to your sacred garden

If you don't already have a place selected, I recommend that you go to Lower World and ask your power animal to help you find/select your sacred garden. Or you could also go to Upper World and ask your teacher, if that feels better. If you do have a place selected, you can go directly there from your starting place in nature. Either way, once you figure out where your garden is, make sure you have a path from your real place in nature.

If you know where your garden is, your intent will be

I will journey to my sacred garden.

If you don't know where your garden is, your intent will be

I will journey to Lower World and ask my power animal to help me find my garden

or

I will journey to Upper World and ask my teacher to help me find my garden.

However you get there, spend some time exploring your garden. Again, the same steps as the journey to Lower World can be used. With most journeys, I begin by journeying to my garden, with the intent that the appropriate guides meet me in my garden to help with whatever goal I have stated in my intention.

Chapter 3—Some Additional Information About Shamanic Journeying

Some additional suggestions

I recommend keeping a journal of your shamanic journeys. It's not required, of course, but it can be helpful. Shamanic journeys can be a bit like dreams, very vivid when you first return, but increasingly elusive as more time goes by. If you feel like you've forgotten something important you can always go and ask your guides again. Also, I find that when I write down a journey, I remember and notice more details. Because we journey outside space and time, an enormous amount of subjective time can pass in one journey. Often it can take longer to write about or describe your journey than the actual journey time.

Time doesn't really exist in shamanic reality. Some people report that a fifteen-minute journey feels like half an hour or an hour; others feel like only about two minutes have gone by. Also, our spirit guides don't really understand time. Their perspective is that time is a circle or a spiral and everything comes back around in a cyclic process. So asking questions about when something will happen will waste your time and confuse your guides. Or, in my case, it doesn't so much confuse my guides as cause them to laugh at me because I know better than to expect an answer to a time question.

When you first start journeying, one or two journeys in a day are plenty. In my classes, I have students do three or four journeys, with the expectation that everyone will experience one or two really good journeys at some point during the day. Shamanic journeying can be like a day at the gym; if you use unfamiliar muscles or work hard, you will be tired afterwards. We are stretching and using our awareness consciously and this requires concentration and focus. There's no harm if you overdo it, but you can feel spacey and tired afterwards and your journeys will become less clear and precise.

If you have difficulty with shamanic journeying

Sandra Ingerman says, "I've never met a person who couldn't journey—but I've met many for whom it took several tries before they could. Keep up the practice. Relax. Breathe into your heart, open all your senses, set an intention, and in time you will be journeying."

If you have difficulty with the first journeys, or just want to increase the ease and vividness of your explorations, I can offer several suggestions. Aside from continuing to practice, you can seek a group to work with. There's something about the energy of a group that allows people to access shamanic reality with far greater ease. In a group, you can work together to set and hold the energy. Or you can select a group with a facilitator.

Another approach I recommend is to journey for someone else, with their permission. Oftentimes, people who struggle to journey for themselves have a far easier time journeying for another person. It may be that there are double the helping spirits involved (yours and those of the person you're journeying for), or it may be that the pressure is off, or some combination of the two. Either way, you may be surprised by how much easier it is to journey for someone else.

If you still have trouble or just learn better in a classroom setting, there are many classes in shamanic journeying throughout the world. As of the writing of this book, I teach classes in the San Diego area and am available to travel to other locations to teach classes. The Foundation for Shamanic Studies also offers excellent classes throughout North America and Europe. A class can be a very good way to learn this skill and it's helpful to have others to compare your experience with.

It's important to recognize when you begin journeying that it may take you a while to get clear, vivid journeys. It's not that the process is particularly complex, but it does use muscles (for lack of a better term) that may not have had much opportunity to develop. You may find yourself tired, especially if you do several journeys in a row when you are first learning. Some people are naturally gifted or have practice using these muscles in other, related ways. But many of us, myself included, develop these skills over time and with practice. If you get nothing beyond a few flashes of disjointed images on your first few journeys, that's a great indicator that you have the potential to develop this skill. With consistent practice, this ability can be developed, even if the initial attempts are frustrating.

I am in no way gifted in terms of physical coordination and have an unfortunate tendency to walk into the door jam instead of through the door when distracted. So I resonate with the analogy of teaching my body to do something physical. It generally takes me three times as long as most people, but eventually my body figures out what I'm trying to get it to do and how to do it. The nice thing is that once you start developing ability in shamanic journeying, progress can be made in leaps and bounds.

Of course, as with anything, it's good to keep track of what you're telling yourself. If you have trouble the first few times and tell yourself you'll never be able to do it, it will make it harder to learn. On the other hand, if you start your journey with an affirmation that the journey experience will be easy and you will get clear information, it can have a great impact. Because our focus and intention are the means by which we travel in the shamanic world, your internal messages will have a great deal of power over your experience and can be used consciously to create the experience you want.

Learning to trust your shamanic journey experiences

Some people ask, after their first successful shamanic journey, "How do I know I'm not making this up?" Shamanic journeying can feel like imagination or visualization. At first, I suggest you simply choose to trust that something is happening and give it some time. I've found that if you do enough journeying, eventually something will happen that's so off the wall, you really couldn't have made it up.

Our spirit guides have a great sense of humor that ranges from punning to just laughing at us, and they will come up with things you wouldn't have thought of on your own. For the scientifically inclined, research on people's brainwaves has shown that listening to a drum with a monotonous beat of 4-5 beats per second, produces theta waves in the brain. So the drumming measurably alters your state of consciousness.

If you wonder whether you're making something up, you can always ask your guides to keep showing it to you. Things created by our guides in shamanic reality will stick around, even if our attention wanders. If we are creating a scene, it requires excellent mental discipline to hold the image for any amount of time. If something sticks around for a while, you're probably not creating it.

The more you use shamanic journeying for self-healing and information, the more quickly you can demonstrate to yourself that this provides a reliable source of information. You might do healing work around an issue and find that it stops being an emotional button. Or you might apply the recommendation of your guides regarding diet and find that they work. There's nothing like a proven track record for allowing you to trust. Besides, if you always get valuable and accurate information, does it really matter if you're "making it up"?

If you're still having serious doubts about whether you're making up your journey, do a journey for someone else, especially someone you don't know very well, with their permission. It's much easier because you won't know the information or second-guess it, you'll just take it in. Important information comes in intuitively in many different ways, so sometimes we get the same information on a shamanic journey that we've been getting for some time in other ways. This often makes us question whether we're inventing the information because we already knew it on some level. Journeying for someone else eliminates the problem of already knowing the answer before the journey.

Of course, even if you are experienced with shamanic journey, there are some journeys that are simply too close and too emotional. When this is the case, you may not be able to achieve the kind of focus and attention required in a shamanic journey. For issues that are highly emotionally charged, ask someone else to journey for you. For example, if your mother just developed breast cancer and gives her permission for someone to do shamanic work, it may be better to ask someone else to do this work rather than attempting it yourself. This is not to say you can't do work for family and friends, but if you are highly invested in the outcome, you may not be able to get clear information.

Apprehension about shamanic journeying

One of the reactions that comes up around shamanic journeying is that of fear. People imagine that with shamanic journeying there is somehow an experience of losing control or losing yourself. In reality, shamanic journeying is a very gentle process. For the first few years after I learned shamanic journeying, I was always completely aware of my body lying on the bed or the floor and of my own consciousness. The process felt very similar to fantasizing or imagining things, just more vivid. It wasn't like falling asleep or losing consciousness. You won't lose awareness or control unless you drift off to sleep while attempting to journey. Once people get past the fear and actually try shamanic journeying, their question frequently changes from the subject of safety or fear to "How do I know I'm not making this up?" As I've done more journeying over the years, I've become less aware of my body while I'm in the journey state. But this shift in awareness has been completely voluntary. I feel more comfortable now, so I go deeper.

Still, some people remain a bit apprehensive about shamanic journeying—it's new and different and sounds really odd. Until someone experiences it, they often still have some apprehension. The last thing I want to do is make anyone more apprehensive. The journeys people experience are always safe and usually beautiful. Yet, for me, there have been a few journeys that have been very uncomfortable and sometimes scary. For example, while doing shadow work to reintegrate my disowned aspects, I came face to face with the part of myself that I had shamed and rejected—not a comfortable journey. It was, however, one of the most powerful and effective journeys for my own healing and growth.

Everyone who has gone through significant healing or growth knows that it can be uncomfortable, painful, and scary. On the other side of a major healing, we experience joy and relief and release. But the actual process is intense. Shamanic journeying is one of the most powerful tools available for healing and growth. So it naturally follows that all shamanic experiences are not going to be about the love and light and boundless joy of playing in the spirit world. Some journeys will be about releasing old pain, changing harmful contracts, embracing disowned shadows, and healing past and present life traumas. These are all powerful and profound experiences but they may not be entirely comfortable.

When you're learning to journey, the first journeys will take you to the places in the shamanic world filled with love and light. These beautiful, comfortable journeys allow you to connect with your spirit guides and learn the techniques for journeying reliably. This allows you to begin to build trust with your guides. When you're ready to do the major healing work, you will know that you are safe, protected, and supported, even if the journey is emotionally tough.

Nevertheless, if you feel too uncomfortable while on a shamanic journey, there are some things you can do. You can always ask your spirit guides to find a softer, gentler way of showing you something or to make their presence, support, and protection better felt. You can return to your sacred garden and continue the journey in that location. There have been times when I stood in my garden (that is, my place of power) and had the person I was speaking to stand outside my garden before I would continue the conversation. Finally, you can always come out of a journey—either through the usual steps or simply by opening your eyes.

I don't believe in spiritual masochism or machismo. There's a place for making an effort to walk through something uncomfortable if it helps you to grow, but if the discomfort, pain, and fear are overwhelming, you don't grow or heal. In fact, you may just add to the existing damage. If you're not ready to walk through something, honor the fact that you're not ready, preferably without judgment. Instead, look for smaller steps to begin addressing the issue.

You can do a journey on what kind of resources the spirit world can offer that will make it safer and more comfortable to heal a given issue before you journey to heal that issue. For example, if it felt overwhelming to address your fear of death, you could ask your guides what resources and lessons they could offer to help you prepare to address that fear. There might be a new power animal that would help you and you might spend a few journeys building a relationship with that power animal and learning to trust it. For your more challenging journeys, go with guides you love and trust and give yourself permission to leave early if it's too much.

Developing your practice of shamanism

Your spirit guides will help you find your way around shamanic reality. The steps I describe will get you to a place of meeting your teacher(s) and power animal(s). For many of the questions you may have about shamanic journeying, it will prove most appropriate to ask your guides. I've studied with a number of different human teachers in my shamanic explorations and invariably, when asked a hard or complicated question, they will tell the person to ask their spirit guides.

I believe that when shamanism is placed in a context of being exclusive, available to only a few special people, or approachable only through very specific routes, the power and force of it is blocked and constrained. Locking shamanism into a rigid, exclusionary tradition can cause the energy to stagnate. So I would urge you to take what I have presented as suggestions, rather than rules, and work out your own approach to shamanic practices with your own spirit guides and teachers. For all that they are willing to communicate with you in within the context and framework of your choosing, if you ask them, your spirit guides will offer you personally tailored shamanic training.

Shamanism is available to everyone who chooses to commit the time and the energy to learning it. A brief survey of the practices of shamanism throughout the world shows that the approaches and practices are as diverse as the people who practice it. Yet, for all its color and variety, ultimately shamanism is being used worldwide for the same purpose: to form a direct relationship with the spirit world, for healing, knowledge, and wisdom, for the individual practitioners as well as for the larger community.

PART 2
THE SHAMANIC WORLDVIEW AND RIGHT RELATIONSHIP

CHAPTER 4—RIGHT ALIGNMENT AND ENERGETIC BOUNDARIES

Right relationship

From the shamanic perspective, all things have spirit and energy and it is possible to interact directly with the natural world around us. The universe is not a passive, indifferent system, but lives and breathes. When you are in right relationship or alignment to the universe, it will actively work on your behalf to protect you, support you, and care for you.

This is different from the Western, Judeo-Christian view of the world. In that mythology, humans were exiled from the Garden of Eden. In many indigenous cultures, the myth isn't that they were thrown out of the Garden of Eden, but that their ancestral lands are their Garden, created by the divine to nurture them.

Alberto Villoldo gives a good example of the difference in worldviews with the example of someone being attacked by a panther as they're walking through a jungle. Both the person from the modern, technological world and the person from an indigenous culture would first seek out the most up-to-date medical treatment available. A modern person might go out and buy a big gun so they could protect themselves in the hostile natural world, or avoid wild, natural places thereafter. The person from the indigenous culture, however, would seek out a shaman to find out how they had fallen out of right relationship or alignment to the world, so that the natural world became unsafe. They would seek to correct the imbalance within themselves. This may be an oversimplification, but I like the way it illustrates the contrasting views and interpretations of the natural world.

Within our modern culture, we seldom have to concern ourselves with being attacked by panthers, but we contend every day with a myriad of complex problems—family, lovers, finance, and careers, to say nothing of traffic. Yet the more I am in alignment with the universe, the more luck and blessings I experience. I find parking spaces effortlessly on busy streets, strangers are kind and go out of their way to help me, I meet the right people at the right time, be it friends, lovers, or clients, and most of all, the things I ask for come swiftly into my life.

When I got ready to set up an office to see clients, the universe moved on my behalf. Out of the blue, one of my dearest friends decided that she was interested in setting up a space with me. We found a space that was exactly the right size, located halfway between our houses, for exactly the amount of money we wanted to spend. We made a list of all the things we wanted to have in our office and more than half came to us as gifts rather than purchases, from a variety of sources. At one point I had gone out with another friend to get a little refrigerator and ended up having to go three places to find it. I commented to him after the second place that it was extremely unusual for something to be this hard and that I wouldn't be surprised if the universe already had a fridge lined up. Sure enough, two days later, there was an offer of a free mini-fridge.

One of the ways we achieve that kind of alignment with the universe, that right relationship, is by healing old wounds and clearing away blockages so that the universal energy can flow freely in our lives. The more we heal, the more energy we can bring to the present moment and the more effortlessly we can manifest our dreams and desires. When our attention is fully in the present, we suddenly allow ourselves to perceive many more choices and options. Shamanic journeying offers a powerful tool for healing ourselves and consciously bringing our lives into right alignment with the universe.

"Negative" energy and experiences from a shamanic perspective

The concept of negative energy is an interesting one. Humans are great at polarization—light and dark, up and down, male and female. Of course, we then begin affixing polarized judgments to the opposites— good and bad, positive and negative. I believe that energy is neither good nor bad; it's just energy, and how it's directed determines how we experience it. Granted, there are energies that nurture us and feel good, such as the energy associated with love, and energies that feel unpleasant, such as the energy of fear. But then, fear serves a very valuable purpose in terms of our survival, so it is not bad, just sometimes misapplied and misdirected.

While energy is not innately good or bad, how that energy is directed determines how we experience it. When energy is made to serve a purpose that it was not intended for over long periods of time, it become stagnant and stops flowing, making it difficult to shift. It's natural to experience the full spectrum of emotions, but if we are angry all the time or if we are never, ever angry, energy is being blocked and not allowed to flow naturally.

When we think about energy, rather than understanding it as positive or negative, it's more useful to look at whether it's in right alignment to the universe or whether it has been shifted out of the most appropriate relationship. When energy becomes stagnant and blocked, it's no longer in a positive relationship to the universe. When energy is applied in right relationship to the universe, it nurtures, heals, flows, and infuses. When it is out of right relationship, it becomes heavy and inert, difficult to access, and almost impossible to use. When people talk about negative energy, they are usually talking about energy that has been misdirected and taken out of right relationship and therefore feels harmful or toxic.

Over time, this blocked energy associated with anger or the lack of anger, for example, will become heavy, dark, sticky, and feel unpleasant. It will begin to block the natural flow of life energy through our bodies and may eventually manifest itself in illness, physical or mental. If anger is used to cover pain or fear, the energy of pain and fear can't be released, so it becomes stuck in our bodies or auras. Most people experience this stagnant, blocked energy as negative.

It's important to differentiate between something that is negative and something that is merely unpleasant or uncomfortable. Many major growth experiences are uncomfortable and often unpleasant. I dislike growing, but I love having grown so much that I embrace and seek out the sometimes disagreeable experience of growing. When I think back on the most traumatic and painful experiences of my life, while I would never choose to go through them again, I wouldn't undo them if I could. While they were awful, I can see gifts that came from every one of them.

For instance, I had an experience with molestation as a child. I would never wish that on anyone and it played havoc with my perception of the world on many levels. But the universe brought me everything I needed to heal from the experience. I retain the gift of being able to better understand, empathize, and hold a space for my clients with similar kinds of trauma to heal because I've walked that path myself. Sharing that experience makes it safe for my clients who've experienced sexual abuse to talk about it and heal those wounds. That horrible, helpless experience as a child of five ultimately afforded a deeper healing opportunity for my clients. The trauma of my childhood advances my soul purpose as an adult.

Maintaining good energetic boundaries

To stay in right alignment or right relationship with the universe it is important to be conscious of the energetic relationship. We need to pay attention to whether we're directing energy in a way that is in right relationship or whether we're misdirecting energy. We are profoundly interconnected on an energetic level. By recognizing this consciously, we have a much greater opportunity to choose what energy we put forth into the world and what energy we take in.

Some people exude light and love—they can walk through a crowded store and leave people smiling as they pass. Other people create waves of drama, frustration, and irritation. Road rage builds up within a dense area of frustrated people, all trapped in traffic. Airports often leave people feeling tired and drained—there's such a mixture of human emotion: joy, dread, goodbyes, hellos, fatigue, excitement. You may have had the experience of walking into a place and either loving it or hating it, before you even looked around.

There are lots of techniques, metaphysical and mainstream, that help people stay centered and not be swept away by what's going on around them. For instance, how many times have you heard, "Take a deep breath"? The more energetically sensitive you are, the more important it is to develop techniques so that the energy around you doesn't have an adverse impact.

Not allowing someone else's anger, bad behavior, or stupidity to ruin your mood or your day is a key to holding onto your own power. If you allow some unpleasant stranger to make you unhappy, you give them the ability (that is, the power) to adversely impact your life. Sometimes it's impossible to avoid being upset, but it's worth considering who you give your power and attention to and whether that's the choice you want to make.

Strong emotions—love, anger, hate, fear—all have energy associated with them. Often when we have strong feelings about something or someone, we unconsciously send energy. When you are feeling very angry with someone, it's important to make sure you don't send that anger at them. Likewise, you don't want to be open to receiving the energy of someone else's anger or obsession that they are directing at you.

A lack of appropriate energetic boundaries can be unpleasant to anyone who is sensitive to such things. People with poor boundaries in ordinary reality also have very poor energetic boundaries. They can fill their immediate environment with their own fear and anger. If a person is exploring metaphysical skills, whatever energy is coming from them, pleasant or otherwise, is amplified.

There are many ways of managing what energy you take in from the world around you. You want to find a way to filter the energy that comes in. That way, you can take in and feel the love and the light around you. It's also good to be able to perceive the unpleasant energy, whether it comes from a person, place, or object. Getting the information that something is unpleasant and perhaps harmful is valuable and important intuitive information. It helps you make good choices to keep yourself safe. But you want to perceive that energy without picking it up or holding onto it.

The simplest approach to controlling the energy you take in is to put up some sort of energetic shields. This can be accomplished in several ways using your intention and visualization. You can simply ask to be protected and shielded when in a place with mixed energy such as a mall, bar, or airport or when you're in a difficult situation. Keep repeating that intent whenever you start to feel energetically impacted by what's around you. You can also visualize a shield of some kind. I see myself surrounded in golden light. Some people use white light. A classic shamanic shield is to see yourself inside a translucent blue egg.

If these don't feel sufficient, do a shamanic journey to ask your guides for help with shielding. There may be spirit guides or power animals that will help protect you or they may make specific suggestions. Various people use herbs, crystals, scents, and charms to keep themselves shielded. Whatever you do, make sure you are very specific in your intent that you are seeking to filter out whatever energies don't serve your highest good. You never want to completely cut yourself off from the energetic flow and it's still important to have the information that comes from uncomfortable kinds of energy.

Another approach is to strengthen your own energetic field. This is especially good because in addition to giving you good energetic protection, it enhances the flow of life energy and increases your vitality and energetic well-being. This can be done simply by visualizing energy from the earth coming in through the souls of your feet and energy from the universe flowing into your crown chakra. How to strengthen your energetic field is a great question to ask your guides in a shamanic journey. If you learn better from books, Ted Andrews has an excellent book called Psychic Protection that deals primarily with managing what energy you take in and strengthening your energetic self. The advantage to this approach is that if you are filled with energy you may not need to create a separate energetic shield. Instead, your strong, clear energetic field will take care of that for you.

In situations where there is a major conflict with someone, I sometimes find myself more apt to dwell on the situation than I would wish. In that case, I start by cutting the energetic cords between us. See the section on cutting cords for more information. If I am still having trouble, I will do a shamanic journey and ask my guides for help with the situation. Often there are lessons that I need to learn from the situation and my guides will help me with those. Our guides also help make sure we're energetically protected.

A high level of energetic sensitivity often feels like a terrible handicap. While those around you may be perfectly happy in a dysfunctional, chaotic situation, the energetically sensitive person goes into meltdown. It's very difficult to be the most energetically aware person in a family system. But energetic sensitivity is a gift; it's just one that takes more effort to make work for you instead of against you. It's important to develop skills to shield yourself and learn how to make sense of the information you get from this awareness. But energetic sensitivity allows you to experience a much deeper level of connection to the world around you and to the people in your life. It's also a gift that is very important for anyone doing healing work of any kind. I haven't always found it easy to be as sensitive as I am, but I wouldn't trade it for the world.

The energy output

It's common to spend time thinking about the energy we experience and take in. We generally spend less time looking at the energy we're putting forth into the world. I remember a conversation with a friend in which she was talking about breathing in fear and confusion and breathing out loving-kindness. I thought she was crazy to be deliberately taking in unpleasant energy but she was adamant that the people who breathe in positive energy and breathe out negative energy have it backwards. I still don't agree with her, but I found the different perspective illuminating.

To be in right relationship and harmony with the world around us, we must pay attention to what kind of energy we send out. As humans, we put energy into the world in a variety of ways. Strong emotions (joy, anger, sadness, love) create an energetic impact on those around us. We also store energy in our bodies. Long after a physical wound has healed, there may be an energetic wound still present. Any kind of emotional trauma may cause us to store the energy stored in our body. When those wounds get nudged, they can become energetic beacons, sending out their energy. While it would be more comfortable if we never had to deal with old wounds and anger and sadness weren't part of our lives, they remain a fundamental and important part of the human experience.

In order to stay in right or harmonious relationship to the world around us when we are angry or sad or experiencing strong, difficult emotions, we need to spare a little bit of attention for how we send that energy into the world. Being honest with ourselves about what we're feeling and experiencing takes a great deal of the potential toxicity out of the energy. If we own that we are angry or even furious, that makes a huge difference.

Choosing a responsible and ethical course of action that honors ourselves and those around us is important as well. We can do a great deal by simply expressing to our guides or the universe that we are releasing this energy and asking that it harm none but instead be recycled and used beneficially. This only takes a moment, a thought or a prayer, yet the impact is huge. Whatever you do, don't hold onto this energy; don't bottle up and swallow your anger or your feelings. But release them with intent that they do no harm, whether or not you take any external action.

It's also important to specifically monitor what energy you are sending out to other people. The more you develop your skills in shamanic energy work, the more likely you are to impact others with your strong emotions. If you find yourself very angry with someone over a long period of time, it is important to keep good energetic boundaries and make sure you aren't sending that energy in their direction.

The romantic obsession is an area where I find I really have to watch my energetic boundaries. When I meet someone and feel all that early energy of attraction and hope and uncertainty, especially if I'm waiting for them to call, I really have to watch that I don't reach out and nudge them energetically. The more metaphysical power and skill you gain or are granted, the greater the responsibility to make sure you aren't misusing it, even unconsciously.

In this case, again, begin with your intent. State the intent clearly that you do not wish your strong emotions, like anger or obsession, to impact the other person in any way. Keep focusing on this intent for as long as the need exists. In addition, consider journeying to ask your guides for help. They will give you more information about the lessons that are in play and your clearest, healthiest path through the experience.

Releasing old energy

When we are going through a healing process, there is a release of energy that has become toxic from our bodies and energetic fields. I once attended a seminar that included intense energy work all weekend long. During the weekend I was so hungry from the work that I ate about twice the amount of food that I usually do with no exercise. Yet, at the end of the weekend, I had cleared so much energetic stuff that I had lost several pounds. I was feeling lighter energetically from the stuff that was cleared, but it also left me physically lighter. Releasing this stagnant energy is one of the best things we can do for ourselves.

In shamanic journeys, my guides often pull out harmful energy that has accumulated in my sacral and solar-plexus chakras. One of my power animals often eats that energy. I thought that was incredibly strange the first time it happened but she explained that it kept me from picking the energy back up. In addition, she simply converts energy that is negative for me back into nurturing universal life energy.

When I do an energy healing session, I call in spirit helpers to recycle the unhelpful energy I remove from my clients. Again, it takes no more than a split second of focusing my intent to arrange for the energy I remove to quickly be returned to its natural state, in which it is neither good nor bad, just life energy. It feels especially right that as I draw out the stagnant energy from old wounds and arrange for it to be recycled, I simultaneously draw in healing universal energy to replenish my client. My engineer side understands that the net impact on the energy of the world is nonexistent, while my client is free of old pain and filled with light.

I highly recommend that as part of your shamanic explorations you go and ask your guides about how to deal with energy that needs to be transformed and transmuted. This doesn't have to be a complicated or elaborate process, but sparing a breath and a thought for this issue will do a great deal to enhance your relationship with the universe. For another source, Sandra Ingerman talks in her books about many different ways that you can recycle what we experience as negative energy into energy that is useful and beneficial.

In the past, we have used the earth to dispose of energy. While the earth may be willing to work with you to recycle energy, it's important not to mirror our physical relationship with the earth in which humans take what they want and then dump the toxic waste. If you put energy you want to get rid of into the earth, put it there with the intent that it be compost, breaking down to nurture the earth. You can send energy into the sun with a similar intent. There isn't a right or a perfect answer, but the more you work with shamanism and energy, the more important it is to spend some time thinking about what you do with energy when you want to get rid of it.

CHAPTER 5—SHAMANIC PERSPECTIVE ON ILLNESS AND DEATH

Thinking about illness

The shamanic perspective on illness is anything but simple. Many people like a cause-and-effect perspective because it allows them to feel safer. But that's kind of like a child pulling the covers over their head to protect themselves from danger. It works great for the imaginary, intangible kind of danger, but isn't a great strategy for immediate physical danger. You can't ever assume that someone is ill because of unresolved emotional or psychological issues, although that is sometimes the case. Nor can you assume that if modern medicine doesn't cure them some spiritual practice will restore them to physical health, although sometimes that happens.

In modern, technological cultures, illness is often seen as an enemy to be battled against. When a person is ill with anything from the common cold to cancer, those around them are full of advice on how to cure the condition. The goal is to make the illness go away as quickly as possible. When attempts to get rid of the symptoms fail, there is often a process of blame-storming: the idiot doctor, the ineffectual medication, or the patient is held responsible. There is a fallacy in assuming that illness can be viewed in simple terms of cause and effect. Yet our scientists keep looking for that information with thousands of studies into what causes heart disease and other illnesses.

There is cultural fear around illness. We invest a great deal of energy in trying to protect against anything that might make us ill. Bacteria and viruses are seen as hostile and everywhere, requiring elaborate measures of sanitation and protection. While it's true that hygiene is never a bad idea, there's also the danger that we manifest our own fears from the stories we tell ourselves. If we are sure something is going to make us sick, it likely will.

Within the metaphysical and psychological communities, there is much discussion of how unresolved emotional or psychological issues lead to illness. While it is true that someone who never expresses anger, for example, is very likely to experience some form of physical illness, the converse is not true. I know people who are whole and healthy and enlightened, emotionally and psychologically, yet have severe physical problems.

I personally feel a great deal of petulance and frustration when I'm sick or in pain, even when I know my own choices, such as not sleeping enough, led to the condition. If I can't see where my choices resulted in my illness, I am truly outraged. I want it to be fixed immediately and so, after treating my condition with conventional medicine, I invariably reach for shamanism and energy healing. The trouble is that they don't always work. I've had times when I've felt physically awful but my energy has been clear and flowing well through my body.

From a shamanic perspective, illness is not an enemy or a failure; it can be viewed as a teacher. Illness invariably brings stress and discomfort, but it also offers opportunities for growth and healing. Alberto Villoldo does an excellent job of putting this into words by talking about the distinction between a cure and a healing. A cure means the symptoms go away, but often the lesson has not been embraced, explored, or learned. In a healing, the symptoms may or may not go away, but the lessons and gifts are embraced and mastered. It's a lovely thing when the physical symptoms vanish during the healing process, but the shamanic practitioner's role is to assist the client in understanding the lessons and gifts of the illness and in healing themselves.

One of the challenges for a shamanic practitioner is to walk that line of being human as well as being a hollow bone or a conduit for information from the spirit world. As human beings, we naturally want our shamanic efforts to lead to the restoration of abundant physical health for our clients. But sometimes that outcome is not in the best interest of the client, as they have made choices and set up contracts to use an illness to learn an important lesson. If we don't honor that, we're not helping or healing.

For example, let's say I have been burning the candle at both ends, as I am apt to do, and I ignore the messages of my spirit guides and my body that I need to slow down, make more time to rest, reduce stimulation. I get sick, as I eventually do if I disregard these messages long enough. If my spirit guides, my own skill with energy work, or a fellow healer were to instantly take away the illness, I would have no incentive to change my behavior. My guides and my own tools help me to move more gracefully through the experience of being sick, but they don't take it away. To do so would deprive me of a valuable lesson.

A concept that has been explored extensively with regards to addicts is that of hitting bottom. Bottom is defined as the point at which things become so awful that the person is willing to walk through whatever it takes to free themselves from their addiction. For some people it's the loss of a relationship or some other similar event. For others, they may be living on the street and still not have hit their bottom.

It's different for everyone at what point things get uncomfortable enough that they are willing to walk through the fear and pain and hard work necessary to grow and change. If you try to help an addict before they hit bottom, you can find yourself enabling them. It may be that your efforts and energy on their behalf keep the full consequences at bay, denying them a much needed wakeup call.

This applies in a larger sense to the lessons we learn as humans. For the really important lessons, the universe will keep escalating the consequences until we hit our personal bottoms. When I overdo, I get tired and less happy with the world. If I keep overdoing I get sick. If I don't stop then, I get really sick. I don't doubt that if I persisted in this behavior over the longer term, I would eventually develop a severe and chronic health problem.

And yet, consequences of actions and choices are only one of many reasons for illness. I had the opportunity to attend a shamanic class on death and dying with an instructor who had significant physical problems. She started the class by telling us that we weren't to worry or be concerned about her—that emotionally and spiritually she was healthy and whole and, as a result, the physical problems were no cause for concern. She talked about one of the gifts being that when it came time for her to die, her attachment to the physical body would be much less.

Because she had mastered the lessons that came from her physical illness so well, what was happening with her physical body did not have the power to shake her from a clear and centered spiritual awareness. When she dies, it will be a clear, awake, and aware process for her, free from fear or attachment. One of our most primal fears, the fear of dying, has no power over her. Furthermore as a teacher, she was showing her students a different way to be strong and whole besides the physically robust style we're accustomed to.

I spent a year volunteering for an organization that provided free services to people with HIV, doing energy healing work. One gift of my time there was the opportunity to meet and work with people who were dealing on a daily basis with the possibility of death as well as a great deal of physical stuff from the HIV and the medications to control it. While I met people who were afraid and angry, I also had the chance to meet people who were incredibly spiritually advanced.

I dislike the practice of comparing spiritual growth as though it were somehow linear or hierarchical, but I was very aware that I spent time in the presence of people who had mastered lessons that I was just beginning to learn. Their spiritual clarity and centeredness took my breath away and I had the chance to offer them healing energy to alleviate some of their severe physical symptoms. I had the strong sense that I spent time with people who had, through their experience with HIV, mastered the life lessons that they had chosen to work on in this lifetime. With that process being complete, they were getting ready to die.

When looking at illness, even, or perhaps especially, life-threatening illness, from a shamanic perspective, think about the gifts and lessons. I'm not knocking the medical model—I'm completely in favor of going to see your doctor if you are ill and taking advantage of the most up-to-date medical techniques available. In an indigenous culture, they worked to stop the bleeding before they pulled out the drums and rattles to summon spiritual help. Modern medicine offers cures and there's great value in that. But after seeing your doctor, whether or not that has provided a cure, it's time to seek healing and examine the gifts and lessons connected to your illness.

One of the major gifts of an illness is the opportunity to slow down and take stock of what's really important. Our bodies are such a critical part of the experience of being human—they enable our physical experience. Yet, so many people, myself included, tend to ignore and neglect them. We get good at being human doings rather than human beings and downtime is the first thing to go. Sitting around doing nothing is frowned on in our culture and yet it can be one of the most challenging and rewarding skills we can master as human beings. Illness gives us the chance to explore downtime.

Illness and physical pain could be considered the master course in maximizing personal power and actively choosing how to walk through the world. In general, I am very happy with my life. My sense of connection to spirit, centeredness, and gratitude are seldom far from my awareness. Yet I'm also aware that I have many gifts—my health is good, my finances are reasonable, I'm surrounded by people who love me, I'm on the perfect spiritual path, and I have a great deal of time and energy to spend as I choose. To master my current state of being with some or all of those things removed is a much greater challenge.

Someone who deals with chronic illness and pain and is happy in their life, who feels connected to spirit and experiences centeredness and gratitude most of the time, has mastered a much more challenging spiritual lesson. And the gift they give to the world is huge. In addition to the love and light and beauty that pour out of them, these are the people who inspire us. When someone succeeds with grace and joy against odds that are much greater than the ones we face, it is much easier to see our own obstacles as manageable.

For a shamanic practitioner or any kind of healing practitioner, there is an additional gift that comes with pain and illness: namely, the chance for a much deeper sense of empathy and compassion for those we help and support in their illnesses. Understanding how exhausting and frustrating and painful and scary physical illness is helps us to hold the people we work with in compassion, without judgment, whether they change and grow or choose to remain where they are.

The shamanic perspective on death

So many people say they want to die quickly, instantly, without a moment's foreknowledge that they have reached the end of their lives. But, working with people with HIV and having known people who died of cancer, I can clearly see the gifts of a slow, lingering death. It gives people the opportunity to reflect and grow. They have the chance to say whatever remains unsaid to their loved ones. They can look at their life and review it and prepare themselves to release their physical body. It can be a beautiful process. It's not this way for everyone, naturally. For some people it's horrible and terrifying and they hate every minute of it.

We can't choose for others the kind of death we would wish them to experience; we must honor the death that each person chooses for themselves. But everyone has a choice and the universe offers the gift of growing and learning more in a few short months than in all the other days of their life every time someone dies slowly. When one is faced with death, suddenly so many of the things that occupy our energy and attention become unimportant, and a slow death offers the gift of weeks or months or years where our attention is focused on what is truly important to us.

In fact, the souls that most often get lost or stuck after death are the souls of people who die suddenly with no warning. Often their consciousness doesn't know that they have died and is confused and frightened. These are the souls that need help to move on. On the other hand, someone who makes peace with the dying process before they cross over is unlikely to need the services of a shamanic practitioner to go to the light on the other side.

If you work as a shamanic practitioner or seek such services, it's important to put aside any tendency to polarize illness as bad, wrong, or unnatural. When dealing with someone who is ill or dying, bear in mind that you seek a healing, not a cure. The recipient may physically improve and they may not. That is not a measure of the effectiveness of the shamanic work. It is common for a shaman to work with a patient through the night and have them die at dawn. While the modern worldview might be that the shaman failed, the shamanic view would be that the shaman helped the person's soul cross over, whole, healed, and intact, rendering the experience of death beautiful and liberating rather than traumatic.

Dealing with loss

In thinking about the shamanic perspective and the idea of being in alignment with the universe, it's important to look at how we view death and loss. Death is a natural part of life. But the more urbanized and disconnected from the natural world our lives become, the harder it becomes to perceive the naturalness of death and dying. I live in San Diego and we barely experience any change of seasons. Sure there are differences between winter and summer in southern California, but if you're not paying attention, they're easy to ignore.

It was easier to understand the process of death and birth as natural and intertwined when we lived off the land more directly and it was part of our everyday experience. In our modern society, we need to remind ourselves, when dealing with death or loss, that while it's very painful, it's not wrong or unnatural, but a fundamental part of life.

Instead of looking at someone who dies young as a failure or a grave injustice by the universe, they could be viewed as someone who has graduated early. If we incarnate to experience certain things and master certain lessons and someone accomplishes that in half the time it takes most of us then, through their death, they move on to the next thing.

When people see the natural process of death as wrong, or bad, or unjust, it makes the grieving process more difficult. But spiritual people can complicate the grieving process for themselves just as much. An intuitive or religious person may know that their loved one is safe and well and happy in the afterlife. Perhaps they've even had a last moment of contact with that person as they came back to visit after dying. So they may decide that it's silly and self-indulgent to mourn. There is somehow an idea that our spiritual awareness should allow us not to experience the hurts of being human.

Loss is painful and grieving is natural and healthy and necessary. You can know with absolute conviction that your loved one is well and that everything is in divine order in the universe and your heart can still ache terribly. Yes, our attachments to our loved ones do indeed cause suffering, but I choose to love completely and trust in my own strength and light in my life that however much a loss hurts, it will ease with time. Just as death is a natural part of life, emotions are natural as well. Honor your own pain and the pain of others when a loss occurs.

CHAPTER 6—ETHICS

A friend of mine once told me that temptation is a wonderful gauge of how inconvenienced we choose to be by looking at ourselves in the mirror. I had just turned down an all-expenses-paid trip to Scotland because I didn't reciprocate the romantic feelings of the person offering the trip. It reminded me that when our ethics really matter is when honoring them requires a sacrifice—giving up something that we desire or accepting a consequence in order to remain in right relationship with ourselves. In this case, I wanted to still be able to say "I don't use people," not "I don't use people except when they have something I really, really want." Still, it was one of the harder choices I've had to make, especially when my reasons were based on something as intangible as my feelings of right and wrong.

Our sense of ethics is first and foremost about remaining in right relationship to ourselves. How well we live up to our personal standard of ethics is fundamental to our sense of self-respect. We should strive to love ourselves unconditionally, but if we don't hold ourselves to an ethical standard, it is harder to respect ourselves. Loving ourselves in the absence of self-respect is difficult.

On a larger scale, our sense of ethics is about remaining in right relationship to the universe. The universe amplifies and mirrors back the energy we put into the world. If we hold ourselves to high standards, offer justice and kindness to those around us, and put positive energy into the world, that energy will come back to us from all directions.

I have found the universe to be very efficient in using questionable ethical choices to advance the growth and lessons of everyone concerned. For instance, if someone is working in a way that encourages people to give up their spiritual power (and money) rather than one that empowers them, that person will connect with followers who need to learn to trust themselves and not look outside themselves. It's not a fun experiences—the followers will feel betrayed and let down. My own experience with an unethical healer was unpleasant enough to make for a memorable lesson. In the sense that it takes two to tango, the universe uses people's misdirected energy to further the positive growth of those who choose to dance that dance with them. It's often painful and costly to learn those lessons and some people choose to repeat them a number of times, but everyone has the potential to learn and grow.

While there doesn't seem to be any judgment on the part of the universe or our spirit guides about crossing ethical lines, there are consequences. Just as the universe will actively conspire on your behalf when you are in right alignment, when you step out of that relationship, you may find that luck and chance are no longer on your side. Crossing ethical lines is one of the fastest ways to take yourself out of right relationship to the universe. Because right relationship is an energetic thing, crossing an energetic or spiritual line will change your alignment to the universe much faster than crossing a physical one. When you misuse power and abilities on a spiritual level, the consequences are likely to manifest immediately. I'm not suggesting that you need to be ethically perfect or always make good choices, but take the high road as much as possible.

The ethics of your spiritual practice will have a profound impact on your life. These ethical standards are more complicated than your physical world ethics. Being responsible in your spiritual practice requires an understanding of other people's rights, boundaries, and existence as spiritual beings. In our physical world, it's somewhat easier to define a set of actions that lead to what many would consider an ethical life. Of course it's a hugely gray area, but it's easier to define the lines—don't kill, don't lie, don't steal—in the physical world. Many attempt to define a similar set of rules and ethics for healing work and spiritual practices. While this is a good start, a rules-based understanding of ethics is insufficient for a spiritual practice that includes influencing the world around you.

We assume that the ability to move energy or perceive things psychically is a gift that comes from being a healthy, evolved, spiritual person. This is simply not true. These abilities are skills that come from time and effort and practice. Also, just as some people are gifted runners, there are people who have a natural ease in connecting to the shamanic world. So skill at shamanic journeying, energy movement, or other metaphysical skills does not mean you or the person you are dealing with is automatically operating from a place of compassion, clarity, and wholeness.

I can't give you a prescription for ethical spiritual practice, but for starters, I will share some of the basic guidelines that are agreed on by much of the shamanic community.

First and foremost, it is important to honor the free choice of others in your shamanic practice. This means not doing work for others without explicit consent. Unless they are unable to provide that consent in an awake state (for example, they are in a coma), asking the person's higher self if you can do work on their behalf isn't an appropriate alternative, in my personal opinion. Nor can someone request work on behalf of another unless that person has given them permission to do so. Remember that from a shamanic worldview, illness and pain invariably comes with lessons and gifts and uninvited interference could deprive someone of the opportunity to receive those gifts and lessons.

When working in shamanic reality, be aware of the things that you have permission to change and the things that you don't have permission to change. If you journey to help someone and they tell you in shamanic reality that they don't want you to do something, it's important to honor it. Everyone, whether in physical or nonphysical form, has the right to decline healing work, even healing work offered with the purest of intent. For example, a client might ask me to contact their long-dead grandmother to heal a wound in the ancestral line that has been handed down for generations. If the grandmother told me in shamanic reality that she didn't want my help, I would honor that. I would also look for ways to make sure that unhealed wound no longer impacted my client without interfering with the grandmother. The universe honors our free choice and it's important that we do the same in our shamanic work.

There's also an ethical question of what you journey on. Using shamanism as a means of finding out about other people when you haven't been asked or invited is inappropriate. Unless you have explicit permission, make sure you are asking your guides to show you information about yourself in relationship to another person, not directly about that person. Anything else is like reading someone's diary without permission or spying on them while they're getting dressed, clearly an energetic boundary violation.

Another issue to consider is that it may not be appropriate or ethical to share information you get on your journeys with others. For example, if I ask a question about what I need to heal in myself related to my relationship with a friend, my guides may show me things about that friend, but it might not be appropriate for me to share that information with the friend. The information I received on my journey would have been different if my friend had agreed for me to journey for both of us. So, in a sense, when you share, you share wrong information. Also, people sometimes take information that people claim is coming from spirit as correct and sacred, without using their discernment about the human source. So, if you share information in these circumstances, you risk someone holding incorrect information as gospel. Bear in mind that, when it comes to painful truths you perceive about others, it is often inappropriate and unkind to share these truths without invitation.

If someone has asked you to journey for them, make sure you differentiate between what you were shown in your journey and what you, personally, might think about it. The clearer and more direct a conduit or "hollow bone" you are able to be when doing work for another, the better. Don't try to choose what they should and should not hear; simply pass along what you are shown for them.

Beyond these guidelines, there isn't a hard and fast ethical rulebook about what constitutes good energetic ethics, so you'll need to spend more time defining and thinking about how this works for you. The good news is that your guides can help you define what is in alignment and what is out of alignment for you personally. The more you stay in right alignment, the fewer bumps you'll hit in life and the easier it will be to deal with those bumps you do hit.

One important premise, in my opinion, is that in the spiritual world, you are dealing with forces and energies bigger and wiser than yourself. There are many ways to understand these larger forces. There is the notion of some kind of God, a benevolent being with a master plan for the whole universe. Or you can consider that your higher self understands the contracts and lessons you are working on in this lifetime. Personally, I have an absolute conviction that the universe is moving in a beautiful dance, that we as humans are all learning and growing.

I believe that my conscious self only gets glimpses and winks from the universe regarding the larger dance. But from any of these perspectives, it is clear that from the human vantage point, we are not capable of understanding the full patterns of the universe and what is best for everyone concerned. We can make guesses and assumptions, but to impose these guess and assumptions on others is misguided at best and damaging at worst.

As you begin to use your shamanic practice to influence the world around you, the ethical questions become more complex. There is a great deal of good that can be done with shamanic techniques for the world around us. Just remember, as you do this, to work for the highest and best outcome, rather than what you, personally, feel is best.

For example, I know of people who work with energy and ritual to change the weather for their convenience. When people attempt to change the weather by force of will, without a strong connection to the natural world, I've seen the weather rebound on them and felt very sorry to be standing near them at the time. But, from an ethical standpoint, these people felt that they were right to impose their will on the weather if they could, without considering that a shift in weather patterns (if successful) might have a damaging effect on other places. This viewpoint presumes that the practitioner knows better than the universe and the planet what is a good idea.

On the other hand, a fundamental role of shamans in traditional societies is being an intermediary and influencing the natural world on behalf of the community. A shaman who is in right relationship to their environment can speak to the clouds and the wind and the rain and ask them to adjust to support the community. This deep and abiding connection, respect, and regard for the land held by traditional shamans and their community was reciprocated by the land itself being prevailed upon to nurture its people.

I had an experience of going camping one rainy weekend in February. While I love the rain, I'm not fond of being wet. As I drove out to the site, I offered up a prayer or request for the rain to stop while I set up camp, if and only if that was in alignment with the universe and wouldn't adversely impact anything else. It poured right until I drove into the campground, at which point the clouds parted and the sun came out. The experience made me feel very humble and blessed.

My point is that it isn't wrong to want the weather to be different or to seek to influence it. But the underlying assumptions and intentions you apply to this goal can put you instantly into an adversarial relationship with the weather and universe. Or your approach can work from sound ethical principles. In either case, the weather may or may not do what you wish, but one approach will definitely take you out of right relationship to the universe; the other will not.

To give another example, when the fires came through San Diego in 2003, it seemed like the whole county was burning. There were separate fires on all sides and many people were evacuated. During this time, I directed energy and did shamanic journeys working for the highest and best outcome. The information I got was that there were some gifts and lessons that came with the fires as well as healing for the land. The fires burned through in such a way that a house would be left untouched while those on either side were reduced to cinders. Some of the gifts included a chance to experience compassion and take care of each other and a chance to focus on what is truly important while releasing attachments to our physical belongings. It was not fun and I would not wish for a repetition, but I was also aware that the loss of life was incredibly low, especially given the vast extent of the destruction. I know other lightworkers were more directive in their energetic efforts, seeking to combat the fires and control the winds directly with energy. I'm not saying this was wrong, but it was a different way of aligning with regard to the fires.

So, as you develop skill and ability with shamanic journeying or with any other spiritual path, spend time and energy understanding and defining your ethics. A more complex understanding of ethics is needed as your ability to impact your own life and the world around you increases. Those drawn to the healing path generally come with the best of intentions. Taking the time to think about ethics will ensure that those good intentions translate into beautiful and positive outcomes for yourself and others.

Chapter 7—Lessons for Working with Others

Once you have mastered the basics of the shamanic journey, you may feel a desire to use these skills to help others. Journeying for information or healing for other people can be immensely rewarding, although it should never be considered an obligation. If you only use shamanic journeying for yourself, that's wonderful. There's no need or requirement that you do healing work with others. Your own increased wholeness will be a gift to the world.

But if you do feel compelled to walk the path of the healer, being of service to others in their growth and healing process, there are some subtle but fundamental lessons you will need to work with. This is true whether you decide to formally do business or never accept a dime for your services. It is also the case whether you work with shamanic journeying, energy healing, psychotherapy, nursing, or any other healing practice.

When it comes to working with others, the energy and information you provide will be used in a variety of ways. Some people will take it and use it for great growth. Others will take it in and keep asking for more without making any changes. We don't actually heal anyone but ourselves; we simply hold a space for others to heal themselves. By holding them and supporting them and reflecting their own great wisdom and power, we offer them the opportunity to heal and grow. I can do exactly the same thing with two clients and one will experience our work as life-changing, while the other will feel little or no result. The best approach we can take in healing work is to see to our own needs and healing first, release attachment to outcome, and ensure that our efforts are in right relationship to the universe.

Healing ourselves first

One of the most important lessons if you wish to do work for others is to attend to your own healing first and foremost. It sounds obvious, but it's easy to look around and find people whose wounds are worse than our own. If you have that impulse to help, you may find yourself spending your energy to help and heal these people, rather than yourself. This impulse often comes from a place of compassion and caring, but it can also have a less admirable motivation.

If you spend a great deal of time working with people who are much more overtly ill and damaged than you are, you will feel healthy and whole by contrast. One of the most effective strategies to avoid having to look at our own issues and pain is trying to fix someone else's. Whether motivated by compassion or avoidance, it's important to be clear that the only person you can heal is yourself, and unless you heal yourself, there is very little you can do that will be helpful for others. I spent years trying to fix and help others rather than healing my own issues, and in the end it wasted my time and alternately enabled and annoyed the objects of my attention.

There will always be people who are more damaged than we are, just as there will always be people who are healthier. Helping others to grow and heal is a beautiful calling. But if you ever find that you are consistently choosing to help others when you need healing yourself, the work you do becomes a misdirection of energy.

You don't have to be perfect or done with your own healing process to work with others. Still, it is wise to have some significant portion of your energy and resources devoted to your personal growth and healing as long as you are working with others. When I began on my spiritual path, I was eager to share my new tools and techniques to help the other people in my life. Every time I attempted to set things in place to start a healing business, I ran into blocks, which pushed me to keep my healing energy and attention turned inward. At the time, it felt like I would never get to work with others. Yet, when things began to line up to start my own practice, everything fell into place effortlessly. As you move forward with your own efforts, pay attention to whether chance and circumstance support or block your endeavors. It's far easier to accomplish things at the perfect time than at your own personal time.

Putting yourself first

If you walk the path of the healer, you must learn how to put yourself first. It can be hard because the impulse to help others who are hurting is powerful and primal. But when you learn to care for yourself first, making sure that all your needs are being met, including rest, recreation, love, and attention, you have the most energy to share with others. When you put aside your needs to be there for others, you begin to run on empty very quickly. Compassionate, giving people can make themselves ill and weary and depressed by taking care of others and seeing to their own needs last.

I often hear the refrain from giving people that they take care of everyone else and no one takes care of them. The best course of action in this case is not to keep giving to others in the hope that one of them will give to you, but to give to yourself. If you meet your own needs first, what you give to others can be done from love, not from a standpoint of bartering or obligation. Martyr caretakers make everyone miserable, including themselves.

As long as I pay attention to taking care of my own needs first, I leave myself the option of putting someone else first from time to time without ill effect. I can choose to take a phone call in the middle of the night or drop everything because a loved one truly needs me and have the reserves to do it. But those events wear me out and afterwards I find I need to pull my energy back to replenish myself.

Learning to receive

If you choose to be of service to others in their growth and healing, you must learn to receive as well as give. For those who walk the path of the healer, giving is often joyful and wondrous. I love the moments of divine alignment when I can say the perfect thing or give a gift of some energy that is exactly what someone needs at that moment. The universe often sets up situations where a small application of my energy is a huge gift for someone else.

The challenging lesson is not how to give, but how to receive. The world abounds with people who are great givers but terrible receivers. For every kind of healing energy you are learning to put out into the world, learn to take it in as well. The healer's path is as much about healing yourself as assisting others in healing and as much about receiving as about giving. If you only learn the giving and the helping parts and not the receiving part, you are not learning the lessons and your effectiveness and personal growth are very much diminished. You want energy to flow through your life in a cycle—energy coming in and energy going out.

Respecting others' choice to heal or not heal

One of the hardest things we face may be watching someone choose not to heal or grow. Oftentimes people dear to our hearts are very wounded. It's hard to truly accept that all healing must be requested and received. You can always offer, but if the person says no that is their right and you must honor it. It's difficult to be detached enough from those you love to honor their right to choose to heal or not heal.

In the grand scheme of things, their illness may contain important life lessons. They may be choosing on a soul level to work through something in a different way. Or they may just not be ready to heal. It's hard for someone who is deeply committed to their own healing to understand how someone else might choose differently. But if you don't honor a person's choice not to heal, you cross ethical lines and take yourself out of right relationship to the universe. Free choice is one of the fundamental laws of our existence and you simply don't have the right to interfere with another person's choices around their own healing or lack thereof. Unrequested healing energy can feel like an energetic attack, rather than a compassionate gesture.

Accepting that there are those you can't help

If you work with others, you will quickly realize that there are people who ask for your help but who you can't assist for one reason or another. Sometimes I get people who want a magical fix to all their problems but are not willing to make different choices or face their pain. There's nothing I can do to assist someone in that situation.

My skill set works best for people who are not in crisis and are reasonably high-functioning. I don't have skills or training to be helpful to someone who is seriously mentally ill. In fact, by working with them, I could do more harm than good and distract them from getting more appropriate help.

It's important to recognize what your gifts are and who gains the most from your service. Not everyone will be able to take in what you have to offer and you won't be able to help everyone. You don't have to work to heal the world single-handed, nor will you ever be the only person and the only option available to someone. Those walking the path of the healer wear all kinds of guises and are everywhere, whether they know it or not. Spend your time and energy with those you are best suited to help. At the end of the session, if you feel joy and gratitude for having the chance to take part in your client's healing, that's a good match.

Releasing attachment to outcome

Another aspect to the healer's path is learning to release attachment to the outcome, thereby honoring your client's free choice and experience. On one occasion, I did a journey for my mother regarding a painful situation. When I started the journey, before my guides did any work with me on the issue, they sat me down and gave me a reminder lecture. In the work that followed, I was to play the shamanic practitioner, not my mother's daughter. As a shamanic and healing practitioner, I recognize the value and release of dealing with old pain directly and the beauty of tears. As a daughter, I hate to see my mommy cry. So my guides reminded me that I needed to honor the fact that my mother had chosen this healing work and it was my place to be of service, not try to protect her, thereby depriving her of this healing experience.

As a shamanic practitioner, you can't give your client the experience or healing or outcome that you want them to have, you can only give them the gift of your services. If you do your part well, in such a way as not to diminish the experience, their experience, healing and outcome is completely out of your hands. We may know intellectually that it's important to let go of the outcome— whether the person heals or doesn't heal—but emotionally it's hard to do. It takes practice, introspection, and regular self-reminders.

Not taking on other people's energy

You may have completely mastered the art of shielding yourself in a busy place or from difficult people, but still find that you have a tendency to pick up unpleasant energy from your clients. This is because when we do healing work, we move into the other person's energetic field and turn our energetic sensitivity all the way up. This helps us to gather intuitive information about how best to be of service.

Many giving, helping people unconsciously hold the erroneous belief that we can carry someone else's energetic burdens for them. After all, if you saw someone carrying several heavy boxes, you might carry one for them, especially if they were physically less able to manage the weight. So, when we see someone hurting, we may reach out unconsciously and pick up some of that energy from them. The trouble is, this only harms us; it doesn't help the other person.

When I first started doing healing work, I had a tendency to be very invested in making my client better. This was partly because I wanted so much for the person to see that I was good at the work and partly because I could see their pain so clearly and wanted to make it better. The result was that I would take on my client's energetic burdens. I'd walk away carrying the energy and weight from what they were feeling. Yet my carrying or picking up other people's energy didn't relieve them of the burden or help them in any way; it just made me weary and sad.

Empathy is a great gift and quality. It's important to be completely present and connected with someone you're working with. But, don't walk away carrying their stuff or feeling their feelings. If someone you love is having a tough time, don't damp down your own happiness. The better an emotional space you stay in, the more you will have to give.

Some final notes on working with others

The people who feel this call to help others heal have a deep, abiding, soul desire to be of service, to help, to heal. The lessons of putting oneself first, healing your own issues before you help others, receiving, and letting go of outcome are contradictory to this intense impulse. When you add in the need to accept other's choices not to heal and the fact that there are people you can't significantly help, it's easy to see why so many healers fail to learn these lessons and burn themselves out.

Learning shamanic journeying and energy healing techniques is easy. Learning to apply these techniques for others in a way that honors both you and others is more challenging. The metaphysical community often talks a lot about these lessons in a way that makes them sound simple and obvious, but while they are fundamental, they are far from easy.

Your guides can help you with all of these lessons. Do a shamanic journey and ask them questions like the following:

- What gets in my way of putting myself first?

- How can I release attachment to outcome?

- What do I need to heal in myself in order to be of service to others?

- What can you teach me that will help me to receive?

- How can I avoid taking on other people's energy?

As you walk through these lessons, be gentle with yourself. No one figures them out overnight. But when you find you're not having a good experience working with others, these lessons are one of the first things to look at.

Chapter 8—Shamanic Fears

Entities

Over the years, I've received a number of calls and questions about bad spirits and entities. I'm reluctant to talk about entities, not because I consider them especially scary but because the concept of ghosts or spirits is so terrifying to many people.

When I first started on my spiritual path and realized that I had helping spirits around me, there was a part of that which felt distressing. I felt like I had no privacy, in my thoughts or my actions. I eventually realized that my helping spirits were not voyeurs and really didn't hear my every thought. They were reading my energy, not my mind, and then only by invitation. But I had feelings of discomfort regarding spirits that I consider utterly benign and completely on my side.

Ghost stories, on the other hand, terrify me. I spent most of my childhood and adolescence avoiding mirrors because of the Bloody Mary stories and to be honest I'm still not fond of mirrors in the dark.

I understand how much irrational fear and unease can be caused by the idea of a hostile or even confused spirit. So, if I go on to say that entities—beings in spirit form that are not guides or helpers—really do exist, there's a chance that I will increase your fear. Before I go on, let me state that reading this chapter is optional. If you believe in entities and want more information about them, or ways to deal with them, read on. But if you find the idea scary and you'd rather not dwell on the notion too much, skip ahead.

If you feel a great deal of fear around entities, I recommend you journey to your guides and ask them for help in releasing or resolving that fear. There may be a power animal that will come into relationship with you that will chase away any and all entities. Perhaps your guides will give you information that will help you release your fear or help you to transmute your fear energetically.

I certainly don't have all the answers about entities, but it is something I've been gathering information about since I joined the metaphysical community. There are spirits that aren't helpers or guides. Sometimes they are the spirits of people who have passed on who got stuck or don't know they've died. Sometimes they're something else. While the fear of unseen spirits is a primal human fear and therefore natural, the fear is not informing us about a real risk. There are plenty of ghost stories where the ghost doesn't actually hurt you; it's just there and scary.

The house I grew up in as a child had a ghost that absolutely terrified me. It was someone who had died, but not realized they had died and, consequently, not moved on. There was nothing malevolent about this ghost, although it didn't like having a couple of small children in its space. As an adult, I went back to the house and helped it move on. I was terrified, but after that, my fear threshold in dealing with entities was much higher.

Entities are almost never bad or evil. Often entities are afraid, confused, or even angry. Sometime the entities that hang around do so out of a misguided sense of responsibility or an attachment to a place that they loved in life. They may not be very pleasant, but they are not evil. Think about an unhappy or difficult person—not evil, but not someone you want to spend a lot of time with.

When someone is seriously unbalanced, they do tend to attract entities. What my guides have told me about the people who call because they feel that they have entities around them is that, while this is true, it is very far from their only problem and really is the least of their worries. When someone is very unbalanced, severely depressed, or very angry and they end up with entities, those entities are no more harmful than the toxic energy that person is giving off, energy that permeates their aura and immediate environment.

Sometimes when people are clear and healthy and energetically bright, they can attract energy hitchhikers that are drawn to their light. If a person is fairly well balanced, the impact will be very mild. In the cases I've seen, there isn't much of an effect, but it does deplete some of the person's life energy. There are entities that are drawn to certain kinds of energy—anger, chaos, drama, fear, etc.—just as there are people who seek out and stir up these emotions. But a person in your life who enjoys stirring up drama and poking at painful emotions will have a much stronger negative impact on your life than entities will.

Nevertheless, it's better to remove any entities, no mater how benign, that become attached to people. Sometime when I'm working on someone, I will see an entity and remove it. I call in the entity's spiritual helpers to assist it in moving on and I reach out energetically and bring back soul parts, as I would in a normal soul retrieval. Once the entity gets back its soul parts, it loses all interest in hanging around my client and moves back into alignment with the universe.

If you feel that there is an entity attached to you or in your space, there are lots of things you can do. You can do a shamanic journey and ask your guides to remove any entities that may be attached to you or in your space. You can also ask your guides why the entity showed up at all.

In dealing with entities, you have the right to command your space. You can call in angels and helping spirits to clear entities, burn sage, or simply assert, "Any thing that is not for my highest and best good, go in peace, but go now and do not return." When you're clearing a space—with sage, with affirmation, or by asking for help from your spirit guides—it's always good to clear unhelpful energy as well as entities.

To clear energy and entities, you can burn white candles. The Virgin de Guadalupe candles are especially good, even if you're not Christian or Catholic. You can invoke her as an archetype that deals with protection. Also, it can be helpful to place bowls of salt around a space. Salt absorbs negativity. Every six months, throw the salt away. Burning an incense called Dragon's Blood is a good way to neutralize negative energy.

If you choose to do more direct work with entities, here are some additional suggestions, just to get you started. More extensive research, with your guides and human teachers, is strongly recommended. Large entities attract other entities. When dealing with them, clear the smaller entities first, then deal with the larger entities.

One approach that people often use with entities is that of being bigger and more powerful. They attempt to forcefully banish entities. I find that a more compassionate approach works better. If you approach entities with force, they react like any being would react to being backed into a corner—fight or flight. They will try to hide or flee or they will resonate with your fear, creating a feedback loop.

I prefer to approach entities as merely spirits or beings that have fallen out of right alignment to the world. My role isn't to banish them, but to be of service in whatever healing they need to move on to a more appropriate place. This means helping souls move on, returning other dimensional beings to their homes, etc. A spirit may need to tell it's story, be informed that it has passed on, or be shown the way to join its loved ones that have gone before. By letting the entity know I'm not seeking to harm it, I gain its cooperation in helping it move on. If you merely banish entities, they leave (or hide until you go away) and remain out of alignment. This approach applies to 95% of the entities that you may run into.

Black magic, curses, and psychic attacks

Most shamanic traditions have a great deal of lore about curses and black magic. Shamans were feared as well as revered for their ability to interact with the spirit world.

There are stories of people being harmed or even dying from curses or black magic. The idea that people could be harmed through magic power is a primal human fear. Look at witchcraft accusations throughout the world, for example. The modern, scientific interpretation of this phenomenon is that if curses work at all, it is because the victim's belief is so strong, they will themselves to death. This can be understood in an anthropological sense as fascinating beliefs of ignorant primitives.

But many people wonder whether black magic and curses really work as they begin to explore and adapt shamanic traditions. Once you have personal experience that the shamanic techniques of indigenous cultures are an effective way to obtain healing, knowledge, support, and protection, it's harder to dismiss the less palatable beliefs out of hand.

In addition to questions from people who are merely curious, I sometimes get calls from people who feel like they are being psychically or energetically attacked. They want my assistance to make it stop and, oftentimes, to retaliate on their behalf— a classic role of a traditional shaman.

My own experience and the information from my guides is that in our modern, technological society, effective deliberate energetic attacks are rare enough to be almost nonexistent. They are possible, but very unusual. In order for such an attack to be effective, many different conditions have to exist.

First of all, the person sending the harmful energy would need to have a great deal of skill. It isn't easy to do and most people who develop a high level of skill understand that to misuse that energy carries some of the biggest, nastiest karmic consequences. Effective black magic takes vast amounts of energy, focus and power. It's like point a gun at your stomach and pulling the trigger in order to hit the person standing 20 feet behind you. You may or may not hit them, but you are guaranteed to shoot yourself. Crossing that line, even with someone who has done horrible things, like a rapist or a child molester, is wrong and will instantly take you out of right relationship with the universe. Instead of the universe working on your behalf, the harmful energy that you sent out will come back to you, magnified.

While not everyone who follows a spiritual path truly evolves as a person, many of us do. The more we grow and release blockages, the more energy is free to flow through us, which tends to make us more ethical people. Sadly, there are some people, not many, but some, who believe they are powerful enough to harm others energetically and are willing to cross that line. But they take themselves much more seriously than the universe does. In short, for an energetic attack to be sent, you need someone with an extremely high level of skill and a complete absence of understanding of the universal laws and right relationship. While there are some people who have one of these characteristics or the other, both are rarely found in the same person.

Furthermore, in order to have a deliberate energetic attack be effective, the intended victim would need to have their power and energetic well-being significantly diminished. If you are filled up with life force energy and your power animals and spirit helpers are doing their job, any negative energy sent at you will be intercepted and flow harmlessly away. What is put out in the energetic world is slow to manifest in the physical, especially if there is an attempt to manifest something that is out of alignment with someone's soul purpose, such as an energetic attack.

So, between the rarity of anyone who would be able and willing to attempt such an attack and your natural defenses, your odds of being harmed by a psychic attack are about on par with being struck by lightening. Sure, it could happen, it's awfully improbable.

Unfortunately, in our modern world, avoiding negative energetic experiences isn't as simple as making sure to keep on good terms with your local shaman so that they won't curse you or let anyone else harm you energetically. While deliberate energetic attacks are very rare and deliberate *effective* energetic attacks are nearly nonexistent, an energetically sensitive person can easily be impacted by the energy we unconsciously send to one another. I've talked previously about how to protect yourself from energy that people unconsciously send you as well as avoiding sending unpleasant energy to other people.

It's important to understand if you feel like you are being psychically attacked, it is very unlikely that the other person is doing it deliberately. Someone's obsession with you can feel like an energetic attack. But don't attribute to malice what can be explained by poor energetic boundaries. This is important because if someone feels that they are being energetically attacked, it's very natural to want to strike back.

Don't go there. The impulse is natural but if you act on it, you will be taking yourself out of right relationship to the universe, relinquishing natural energetic protection, and infusing your own energetic environment with your negative intentions. Because strong emotions can send energy, even if we don't mean them to, be very clear that you do not intend to send these emotions. If you do, you will do yourself vastly more energetic harm than the other person could ever have a hope of doing to you.

Again, even if you are utterly convinced that someone is deliberately seeking to harm you, don't retaliate. In times of stress and unease, when we are afraid, it becomes harder to perceive clearly into the unseen world. And if there is negative energy coming from another person, your energetic participation will feed and fuel the energetic exchange between you. If you attempt to throw negative energy at someone, you will be personally, irrevocably responsible for the karmic consequences of that action, regardless of what they did first. There's no sense of time in shamanic reality, so your soul record only shows what you did, not what was done to you first.

I had the opportunity to work with someone who felt he was being psychically attacked. His auric field was a mess, filled with rips and holes. There were scary entities all around him. What the guides said was, "Tell him he needs to stop doing black magic." It wasn't that anyone was attacking him, but his belief and participation in this type of energy attracted lot's of nasty things. Because he needed to learn the lesson about not doing black magic, his guides were not protecting him.

In a situation where you feel psychically attacked, focus your energies on staying in right alignment and let the universe take care of the other person in its own time and its own way. Don't sign up to share the nasty karmic fallout that is headed their direction. The universe is paying attention and it's much bigger and better at sorting these things out. It just may not happen as quickly as we would wish. Consider also that you can just stand by, strength your own energy protections, and let the person drain their power and energy in a fruitless effort.

If you do feel as if you are being attacked energetically, by all means go and ask your guides what's going on and what you can do about it. They will help you find an ethical and appropriate way to feel safe and protected from this kind of harm.

On a final note, I have known people who created an experience of being psychically attacked through their fear and obsession. In such cases, the person's fear and disowned aspects caused them to feel that a psychic attack was happening, but it was entirely of their own creation. We can, after all, create our own reality. If you feel that the universe is out to get you or that those around you mean you harm, you will create that reality for yourself. It's easy to feel afraid of being harmed through metaphysical means—that fear caused people to burn their neighbors at the stake. But while we can recognize that it is a fundamental and natural human fear, we get to choose how much attention and power to give to that fear and how to act on it.

If you would like additional information about entities and psychic protection, I recommend Ted Andrews' book, Psychic Protection.

PART 3
MORE ADVANCED SHAMANIC EXPLORATIONS

Chapter 9—Further Shamanic Explorations

Getting answers to your questions

Shamanic journeying is perfect for getting information about the kind of questions that you lie awake at night wondering about. It can be used to get more information about a problem or experience. Whether you can't stop thinking about how to deal with a financial situation, your romantic prospects, the argument you had with your wife, boyfriend, or co-worker, why life includes illness, what can be done to help your stomach troubles, the meaning of life, or any of a multitude of other questions that you may be turning over in you mind instead of resting, shamanic journeying is helpful.

For example, when it comes to dating someone new, I find that it's very easy for me to spend a great deal of time thinking, wondering, hoping, and generally obsessing. While most people ask their friends' opinions of the new object of their affection, I ask my spirit guides. My guides will show me if there's a past life connection or unfinished karmic business. They will show me the lessons that I am working through with this person. They will show me the gifts the relationship offers and they will recommend things to keep in mind as I go forward to have the smoothest, most productive experience. In a sense, they hold up a mirror that allows me to see myself in the exploration, including the reflection of all the energetic themes and connections that are in play. As a relationship progresses, my guides help me to understand which issues are mine and which are the other person's and to understand if and when it's time to move on. Voila, no more sleepless nights.

So, if your spirit guides know so much and are so great about answering questions, can they tell you the winning lotto numbers or what will happen next in the stock market? Alas, no. Part of it is that our spirit guides aren't really predicting the future; they simply perceive energetic relationships, themes, and connections between people and events and can show them to us. Part of it is that our guides won't give us any information that isn't in our best interest to have. I know one person whose guides play with her when she asks the winning lotto numbers by giving her most, but not all of the numbers. Like mine, her life path and life lessons would not be advanced by winning the lottery, so her guides won't give her that information. But even if your guides were willing and able to tell you the winning lotto numbers, time doesn't exist in the same way in shamanic reality. A guide who sees time as a spiral that can be traveled forward or backward isn't going to have reliable information about our linear, one-way time. You might be given the winning lotto numbers for a year ago or for five years in the future.

When you ask your guides about future outcomes, they will give you an answer based on how the energy lines up at that moment in time. There's always opportunity to change a likely outcome—applying energy and attention will change how the energy lines up, and thus the outcome that is unfolding. The shamanic perspective is that the energetic world is the blueprint for what manifests in the physical world. So, by asking questions and understanding what outcomes or energetic themes are in play, we create the opportunity either to consciously support what we are manifesting or to make changes so that we manifest a different outcome. When you ask your guides about the future, they will answer based on the snapshot of your energy at the time of the question. Since that future is subject to change if you make different choices or bring in different influences, it's always good to ask important questions again over time to see if the answer has changed.

Some of the many questions your guides can provide information about include the following:

• What are the next steps on my spiritual journey?

- What kind of diet should I be eating for optimal health?

- What does my body want me to know?

- What gifts does this guide bring to the relationship? What are they here to teach me?

- What obstacles are in the way of reaching my goals?

- What do I need to heal in order to have a fulfilling relationship with a lover?

- Why am I having such intense conflict with this person?

- What is the gift or lesson in this illness, conflict, problem?

- What can you show me about this relationship?

- Which past life is most strongly impacting this lifetime?

- How can I go about healing this issue?

- What was the meaning of this dream?

When asking questions, make sure you approach it in the most ethical way possible. You have the right to ask for information about yourself, but it's important not to ask for information about other people without their permission. For example, you can ask, "Why am I having so much conflict with this person and what can I do to correct it?" or "What lessons am I working on with this person and how can I move through them gently?" However, it's inappropriate to ask, "Why is my spouse so angry?" or "How does this person feel about me?" In other words, you have every right to ask questions about yourself, but you do not have the right to ask for information directly about another person without their consent.

If you have a complicated, life-changing kind of decision to make, it can be good to take multiple journeys on different aspects of that question. For example, if you were attempting to decide whether to have an elderly parent move in with you, you might journey on "How would doing this affect my life?" "What would be the impact on our relationship?" "What challenges and lessons might this bring to me?" "What would be the gifts of making this choice?" "What would I have to give up if this happened?" It's good to break big questions or complex questions into smaller, more manageable questions.

Working with the answers

With shamanic journeying, our guides often provide information symbolically. For instance, my guides will often show me a good relationship as a dance—whether they show me that I'm waltzing or dancing swing includes information about the relationship. For me, the visual, symbolic image allows the message to sink in much deeper. The only drawback of this is that sometimes I have no idea what my guides are trying to show me. When this happens, I ask to be shown in a different way. My guides have always been very patient and creative about coming up with different ways to convey the information they want to communicate, no matter how many times I've needed to ask to be shown in a different way.

Another thing to bear in mind about questions asked of spirit guides is that things manifest faster in the energetic world than in the physical world. So the energy may be completely in alignment for a certain outcome, but it may take longer to manifest in the physical world. As Sandra Ingerman points out, "soon" in shamanic reality could mean today, next month, in five years, or next lifetime.

If your guides show you that everything is in alignment for the new job you want to find, you can keep asking what the best steps are for you to take now, but don't be discouraged if the energetic takes some time to manifest in the physical. Make sure you keep working toward your goal in the physical world as well as the energetic. The good news is that things seem to be manifesting much faster these days.

In general, spirit guides give us more information and show us what things look like energetically. They don't tell us what we should do. Shamanic information is more about cause and effect, energetic relationships and webs, where we've been, where we are, and where our choices are leading us. There is an enormous amount of information available to us from our guides in the shamanic world. This information can be immensely helpful in making major life decisions. However, it is vitally important that we own complete responsibility for our life choices.

Doing something because "spirit told us to" and then refusing to take personal responsibility for the consequences is a misdirection of energy. We as humans often miscommunicate when speaking the same language; it's even easier to misunderstand or misinterpret information from the shamanic world. So always run any information you receive through your own discernment and consciously decide whether or not to make it your own. Our hearts are very wise and will resonate strongly with our personal truth.

Dancing your power animal

Dance is found in shamanic cultures through the world. Dancing induces an altered state of consciousness, allowing the dancer to access the shamanic world. In particular, dance can be used to connect more fully with your power animal in a practice known as dancing your power animal. It is believed in traditional societies that when you dance your power animal, you give it a taste of being in a physical body, thereby compensating it for protecting and helping you. My power animals offer a different perspective. They are very clear that I'm not required or expected to dance them, but that if I choose to, there are many gifts that they can offer me. They tell me that dancing power animals is not something to do for your power animals but for yourself.

When dancing a power animal, start with a drumbeat that's slower than the one for shamanic journeying. Unlike when you engage in shamanic journeying, you can drum or rattle for yourself while dancing and adjust the rhythm as feels appropriate. Begin to move with the beat, walking or dancing slowly. Focus your intent as to which power animal you want to dance. As you move in time to the beat, you enter an altered state and eventually you will feel prompted to move in certain ways that are like the animal you are dancing. It may take a little while and it definitely requires letting go of feelings of self-consciousness. But dancing your power animal allows you to fully access the life force and energies of your power animal even as it deepens the relationship. When you dance the energy of different power animals, their individual energy becomes familiar and can be accessed and recognized in shamanic reality as well as in everyday life.

Dancing power animals and dancing to achieve an altered state are a wonderful practice, but can be hard for a modern practitioner to get into. Lying quietly while journeying may feel strange, but you don't have to worry about what it looks like to others because your experience in shamanic reality is yours to share or not share. But if you dance with other people or even alone, you must be willing to set aside some fear and self-consciousness.

In one class, we took a journey to meet a new power animal. I was rather bemused when the power animal that came forward was a kangaroo. All the more so because it wanted me to dance it and I wasn't too thrilled with the idea of bouncing up and down. In general, I prefer to journey lying down. But, according to this new guide, I was missing an important part of the shamanic experience.

When I danced the kangaroo, I felt the energy rush through my body. Fatigue fell away as this vital energy moved through my body. There was the instant when I fell into the experience, setting aside thoughts of looking foolish and undignified. My consciousness shifted out of my head, stilling my inner monologue, until I was completely present in my body and in the moment. I wasn't just accessing the primal power of the kangaroo; I was accessing my own personal primal power, going back to a time before I began to live more in my head than my body.

For me, the need to dance power animals went beyond the basic importance of the shamanic practice. In addition to showing me how I might dance the energy of a kangaroo that did not include a human pogo stick imitation, the kangaroo pointed out that this is an aspect of my spiritual growth that could use more attention. While I integrate my spiritual tools and gifts very well into my mental/emotional aspects, I tend not to blend the spiritual with the physical. While my spirituality was a large factor in deciding to make exercise a regular part of my life, it remained a means to an end, not something I did for its own sake. By my failing to integrate the physical with the spiritual, my body remained somewhat disowned and uncelebrated. For me, no matter how often I journey or how effortlessly I move healing energy, my spiritual practice will be incomplete without some form of spiritual movement.

Shamanic journeying and dreaming

Clients often ask me about how shamanic journeying compares with dreaming. Many people tell me about dreams that have included powerful experiences with animals or spirit guides and dreams that have offered valuable information. When I began working with energy healing, my dreams shifted dramatically. Following my first Reiki attunement, my attention was very much occupied with connecting to my spiritual guides. While it would be several years before I mastered the art of hearing my spiritual guides at will, they wasted no time in joining me in the dreamtime.

It's funny in retrospect, because at the time I was so frustrated that I didn't instantly have the ability to understand my spiritual guides. Yet, night after night, I had vivid, intense, Technicolor dreams. Then I discovered shamanic journeying and the great joy of being able to talk directly to these seemingly elusive guides. As I explored the shamanic world, I came across spirit guides and power animals that I had met in dreams years before. It quickly became clear to me that I had been visiting my guides in shamanic reality long before my first deliberate shamanic journey.

During a shamanic journey, some of your awareness leaves the body and travels elsewhere, across space and time. Likewise, while we are dreaming, our awareness often roams away from the physical body. The difference, of course, is that a shamanic journey is a conscious, self-aware experience. We decide to take a shamanic journey, select our intent for the journey, and use our focus on that intent to get us where we want to go in the shamanic world. In dreaming, on the other hand, with the exception of lucid dreaming, the conscious, self-aware aspect is not part of the process. Because we're not consciously directing our dreaming journeys into the shamanic realm, the experience will be more elusive and harder to understand and recall.

The line between shamanic dreaming and shamanic journeying is a fine one. Often when people are tired and trying to journey, they aren't able to focus and they drift into a dream state. The images that they get seem more disjointed and are harder to remember. When this happens, it isn't bad; it's just not shamanic journeying because you are not able to consciously engage in the experience. While dreams don't give you the same opportunity to consciously choose where you will go and who you will see, we don't need any training to cross into the shamanic world in dreamtime. It is something that happens naturally to human beings.

I don't believe all dreams are unconscious journeys into shamanic reality. Our dreams serve many functions and I am only addressing one small aspect in this section. But when our dreams take us into shamanic reality, there are opportunities to receive spiritual guidance and healing. For example, people often meet their power animals in dreams. Horses, one of my power animals, sometimes appear in my dreams. When they do, there's an intense love for the horse combined with a feeling of soul longing related to the connection to the horse. The horse is the power animal that carries me around shamanic reality and it seems that in these dreams, the horse takes me to experience things that I can't understand or contain when I'm in my waking human state. The dreams that include my guides and power animals have a powerful emotional content. When I awaken from these dreams, there is often the sense of having been away rather than sleeping. Waking up feels like my attention has shifted from one reality to another, not like a dream falling away.

As with conscious shamanic journeying, there is an opportunity to set your intent about your dreaming journeys. We are very protected in these kinds of experiences, but if you have any concern for your safety, you can ask your angels, guides, power animals, or higher self to ensure that you are completely protected. Likewise, you can invite your guides to communicate with you in the dreamtime merely by focusing on your intent before you fall asleep. This creates an opportunity for your guides to connect with you on very deep levels of your being. I also find that, minus the conscious filters, my dreamtime journeys tend to have a more vivid emotional landscape and stay with me longer and more intensely than many of my conscious shamanic journeys.

You can use normal shamanic journeying to explain, remember, or finish a dream. I had a dream once in which I used my greater power as an adult to abusively impose my will upon a child. In the dream, I was horrified that I had crossed that line, even through the child forgave me in the dream. I was told in the dream that I needed only to remember that I had the potential to cross that line. Still, I was still very upset when I woke up. I did a shamanic journey to understand that dream and my guides told me that because I'm thinking of having children, I'm learning and exploring lessons in my sleep. I wasn't intended to remember the dream, but I had set my alarm an hour early, so I woke up in the middle and remembered. I was grateful that I had the opportunity to discuss the dream with my guides.

The only downside to traveling in shamanic reality during sleep is that if you spend a great deal of your night roaming outside of your body, you aren't resting in the same way as if you were just sleeping. Many people have had the experience of waking up from vivid dreams feeling tired. If you find that you travel a lot in your sleep, you may need to allow extra hours asleep so that you get the rest you need. It can also be useful to sometimes ask that you simply rest in your sleep and not travel anywhere when you start to feel worn out. Our guides love to communicate with us, but they don't always completely understand the human experience and the body's need for rest.

Connecting to the natural world

Shamanic cultures believe that everything in the natural world is alive—the rocks, the trees, the wind, and the stars. It follows that they developed techniques to go and interact with spirit of things in the natural world. Even in our modern, technological lives, we interact with the world around us at every moment on an unconscious, energetic level.

I live in San Diego and I enjoy the abundant opportunities for human connection that this city offers. Yet, when I get away from the city, out in nature, there is a psychic quietness that feels wonderful. It's like a background buzzing noise that you're not aware of until it suddenly stops.

When I'm out in nature, there are some things I do to honor the world around me. I try to become quiet within myself and listen to the energy of the place. I open myself up to the gifts and the healing that I find there. As I look around, if I find a rock or a feather that speaks to me, I ask before I pick it up. One friend of mine described being out in the desert and picking up a piece of wood without asking. Within a few minutes, she had tripped, stumbled, and run into a cactus. The desert suddenly became prickly and unfriendly. After she apologized and returned the piece of wood, everything smoothed out again. This is a classic example of what happens as you step into and out of harmonious relationship with the natural world.

Many indigenous cultures have rituals like leaving tobacco and other gifts to honor the natural world. I tend to simply send out the energy of my gratitude and appreciation for the place. It seems that seeing a place in nature, loving it, and thanking it with sincere intent is enough. Sometimes I will pick up trash that I find there. Most people enjoy seeing new places, but when you actually feel the energy of the place reach out to welcome and embrace you, it makes for a vastly richer experience. As with everything in shamanism, simply focusing on your intent to honor and connect with a new place will form a bridge.

When you do healing or energetic work in a place in nature, it is best to acknowledge the spirit guides and guardians of the place and ask their permission. You may or may not feel that you get a clear answer, but asking sets up a different kind of relationship with the place. If a guest in your home asked if they could get a cup of water, you would gladly offer it to them. But if someone simply started looking through your cupboards and got a glass of water the first time they came into your home, you probably wouldn't appreciate it. Consider similar good manners when dealing with the natural world.

You can also do a shamanic journey to meet the guardians of a new place. On a trip to Scotland, I did a journey to meet with the spirits of the land. They appeared as a man and a woman but made it clear that this was not their natural form, merely a guise they adopted so I would feel comfortable speaking to them. They told me I was most welcome. I asked permission to take away rocks that I might find and they told me that I had to discuss that with the rock in question. They invited me to help with some spirit release work and that was profound experience. The entire trip was vastly enhanced by my ability to experience the physical places of power in the United Kingdom as well as what those places are like in shamanic reality. I still go back and visit Britain in my shamanic journeys and I traveled there in shamanic reality long before I first set foot on British soil.

You can use your shamanic journeying skills to actively enhance your relationship to the natural world. One excellent way to do this is to do a journey and ask your guides to help you be of service to the natural world in some way. Sandra Ingerman talks about doing soul retrieval work for places in nature that have been misused. I have done journeys where I helped to energetically transform and transmute pollution and damage to the earth. Your guides will be able to teach you things to do to help and heal the earth if you just ask them. Putting forth some time and attention to being of service to the natural world puts you into an abundant energetic relationship.

When doing healing work for the earth (or anything for that matter), do it with love and compassion. If you dwell on how the earth has been misused or damaged, you may find that you take on that energy or begin to feel depressed or heavy. For the time you're being of service, it's important to put aside the anger or resentment that you may feel about abuses that people have inflicted on the earth. Bring your best intentions, your love and your light, and offer them in service to the natural world. The energy will be magnified and reflected back.

Journeying to be of service

Shamanism offers many opportunities to be of service to the world. Alberto Villoldo talks about how, for a shamanic practitioner, the spirit world will always answer when you call. I have never had a journey when I asked to meet my spirit guides and they didn't come. There have been times when I wasn't in a space to take in or make use of what they offered, but they always came. They never take a message and get back to me or tell me they have other things going on. When I call, they come.

Shamanic practitioners often find a growing impulse to be of service in return. There's not an obligation to do anything or answer when the spirit world calls to you, but there are huge gifts if you choose to respond. It can be as simple as holding the light for another person with a smile or a compliment. Often as I move through the world, I perceive opportunities to send good wishes, prayers, or energy toward a situation that crosses my path. This doesn't have to be elaborate, and seldom requires great sacrifice, but part of how I stay in right relationship to the universe is my awareness that I want to have a positive impact on the world around me.

Being an engineer, I look for leverage points. Archimedes said, "Give me a lever long enough and a place to stand and I will move the world." I am constantly looking around for opportunities where a small word or action on my part will have huge benefit for others. You can find the opportunities all around you simply by paying attention. But when you step up to be of service to the world, there are a few things to keep in mind to maintain that right relationship and good alignment.

First and foremost, remember to honor yourself. If you are depleted, meet your own needs before you try to help other people or the world around you. When I've done a shamanic journey for someone else when I needed some healing work myself, my guides have grabbed me and assisted with that before they even talked about the other person. Sometimes when you're in process it can seem endless, but you have the most power to impact yourself. You have more to give to the world from a place of strength and abundance than if you're trying to help others without bothering to stop your own bleeding.

People give for a number of reasons and there are many ways to give and they are all valid. But when it comes to enhancing universal alignment, the best reason to give is that it feels wonderful. Giving out of guilt or obligation will do nothing to enhance your relationship with the universe. If you feel resentful or drained from the things you give, you actually take yourself out of universal alignment. It is very important to make sure you are giving from a place of abundance.

We all know activists who are filled with anger at the conditions they strive to change. They may look at themselves as martyrs, making outrageous sacrifices for their cause with a great deal of drama. Often they are furious with the other people for not caring about their cause as deeply as they do. Take vegetarians, for example. There is one kind of energy when someone says that they are choosing not to eat meat because they feel in better alignment with the world when they make that choice. There's a completely different energy when someone chooses not to eat meat because eating meat is wrong and cruel and only bad, selfish people eat meat. I'm not sure whether angry activists are effective or not. There is a place to be angry and feel strongly that the world isn't as we choose and it is right to strive to change it. But if you seek change from a place of anger rather than joy and compassion, I'm not sure it works.

When we're working in shamanic reality, the notion of "Be the change you wish to see" should be a guiding principle. If you do a journey to help heal the earth, don't bring your anger and outrage on the journey; instead bring in love and compassion and a desire to be of service. Because things in shamanic reality are all about energy, an angry shamanic practitioner trying to effect change can do more harm than good. If you are angry to the core of your being about human rights violations or racism or some other issue and can't put that aside, take action in the physical world, not the shamanic world. Or ask your guides to help you work through your anger before you attempt a journey.

If you do a journey to be of service, look to your spirit guides for advice and help on how big a piece to bite off. For example, when the tsunami hit in December 2004, I did shamanic work to help with the situation. I didn't just head over there in shamanic reality, but went to my guides to ask them what would be best. They took me there to help souls move on, to retrieve lost soul parts, to calm the fears of those who had died, and to soothe and dissipate the energy of fear, shock and loss. However, after a very short time of my doing this work, they indicated that it was time for me to leave. The energy was so chaotic and difficult that I could only work for a short time and be energetically protected. It wasn't for me to do all the work that needed to be done, but I had the chance to help with an appropriate piece. The help and guidance of my spirit guides was key in this experience.

CHAPTER 10—SHAMANIC WORK FOR SELF-HEALING

Energetic healing in shamanic reality

Keeping ourselves fully charged up energetically and replenishing our energy when we get depleted is important. Our spirit helpers are adept energy workers and can be of great assistance in this. Such energy healing can range from clearing our bodies and auric fields of any unpleasant energy we've picked up to healing deep, abiding wounds.

The process for receiving an energetic healing in shamanic reality is simple. Start by setting your intent regarding what you want to heal or shift. It could be a specific issue, such as an experience of emotional abuse or the pain in your back. You could ask that energetic blockages in your body be cleared away. Or you can set a general intent, such as to have your energy replenished and the unhelpful energy cleared away. Then, with your intent firmly in mind, go to your garden and as your guides for help.

When my guides pull out energy from old wounds and blockages in my body, the energy looks thick and black and sticky. Sometimes when you release blocked energy you've been carrying for a long time, there is a hollow feeling where that energy used to reside. We can even pick that energy back up again for the familiar feeling of fullness. So if your guides remove energy, they will usually find a way to replace it with new life energy afterwards. While in my sacred garden in shamanic reality, my guides sometimes have me lie in the sun to soak up energy or lie in the water. Sometimes they will have me sink into the earth.

I have found that when I need to cry, shamanic reality is a good place to do it. Sometimes I'm not even in touch with that need until I arrive and one of my guides holds out their arms and embraces me. For me it's the best of all worlds. I am self-conscious about crying in front of other people for fear of making them uncomfortable. But crying alone can be lonely. So, with my guides to hold me, I'm not alone nor do I have to worry about anyone being uncomfortable. My guides help me release energetically whatever I need to let go of with the tears. There's just no downside to feeling unconditionally and completely loved when you're hurting.

Sometimes I come home feeling worn out. Often times, because my goals so far exceed my time and energy, I am unable or unwilling to stop and rest for very long. In that case, I often use a shamanic journey to replenish. It's the ultimate power nap. Sometimes I curl up in my sacred garden and sleep for the length of the journey. At other times, my guides will help to clear and realign my energy field. Water is especially powerful: they often direct me to swim in a pool or stand in a waterfall that is in my sacred garden.

The full gamut of energy healing is available in shamanic reality. Spirit helpers can reweave damage to the aura, cleanse and re-energize our bodies and energy fields, and help us heal core level wounds. That being said, I still find value in working with human facilitators. There are wounds and growth opportunities that benefit from a human touch and connection. But having both available, rather than one or the other, gives us a much greater range of healing opportunities.

Cutting cords

In one of the classes that I took, we performed an exercise that illustrates the complexity of human energetic relationships. This is how it went. Imagine that you're one of a dozen people standing in a circle. Each of you receives several pieces of string. In turn, each person hands one end each of their strings to other people, until everyone is connected to a complex, interwoven web. Then each person in turn hands their strings to the person next to them and steps into the middle of the circle. Imagine how it feels to stand there, surrounded by strings on all sides. If you hold perfectly still, it's not so bad, but when you try to move, the strings bind you in place, making movement (change) nearly impossible.

The exercise with the string is a good illustration for what is going on with the energetic cords that bind us to people, places, and experiences. These energetic cords are created by our thoughts and emotions, especially strong ones. We send them to others and others sent them to us. Fervent prayer for a loved one's safe return, fury at a situation or person, intense nostalgia for the summer when you were nine, all create energetic cords. The thought or emotion can be pleasant or painful, either one will create cords. Furthermore, others can send cords to us with their strong thoughts and emotions. These energetic cords can be viewed as a kind of psychic connection and allow the exchange of information and energy.

Cords, in and of themselves, are not bad. The energetic cord that connects us to our higher self is absolutely vital to our well-being. In your spiritual practice, you may consciously establish cords connecting you to the earth for grounding and to the universal source for life energy. However, when we maintain energetic cords connecting us to someone we're angry with or to a painful event from the past, those sap our energy. If the moment the thought or memory flits through your mind, your emotional state shifts, it's a fair bet that you have a cord there.

If the cord is providing you with joy and light, such as the thought of someone you love or a wonderful experience, you may choose to keep it. On the other hand, if the thought of your ex or your mother or a time in junior high makes you afraid, angry, wounded, or depressed, cutting that cord is in your best interest. I highly recommend cutting cords with ex lovers and former spouses when the relationship is over. Otherwise, even though you've separated, you may still feel bound to that person. It's also helpful to cut cords sent to you by other people.

Some people make a compelling argument that all cords except the one to your higher self should be cut regularly. They point out that this frees up the most energy for the present moment and provides that greatest freedom to grow spiritually and change. These people are generally following a Buddhist-type path, in which cutting cords is part of the practice of nonattachment. But this approach can be disruptive if you're not on a Buddhist-type path of nonattachment. One friend of mine experienced a disruption in her connection to her partner and children after she cut cords to them. While cutting the cords freed up energy and made her less attached, it was not in line with her spiritual choice to remain closely connected to her family members. Personally, I choose to keep some of my cords—specifically the love-based cords to a select group of people in my life.

So let's say that want to keep the love cord with someone in your life, but they also make you crazy and you could do without the energetic cord this creates. It's possible to keep the cord that's based purely in love and cut or trim away the cords that aren't. Psychologists talk about these complex relationships to loved ones as multi-strand relationships, as opposed to single-strand relationships, such as you might have with your bank teller. Our relationships to our close friends and family are multi-strand relationships and we develop many different kinds of cords for that reason. Cutting all but the love cord between you and a loved one can help to establish cleaner, clearer energetic boundaries without disrupting the love connection. In fact, it can bring the love aspect of the relationship to the forefront in dealing with the other person.

When it comes to events or experiences, cutting cords can be very valuable. Conventional therapeutic means such as hypnosis, EMDR (Eye Movement Desensitization and Reprocessing), and NLP (Neurolinguistic Programming) can be used to keep the memory of a traumatic experience but remove the emotional content. Cord cutting can accomplish something similar. When you cut the cord to a memory, good or bad, you don't give up the memory of the experience; you just don't have a direct, energetic link. It's the difference between keeping an object always in front of you or in your hand and putting it away, neatly and carefully, to get out again when you choose.

Another area where cutting cords can be useful is with loved ones who have passed on. This can be hard to do when you're first grieving for a loss. Cutting the cord to someone who has passed on frees the deceased's soul to move on and the living to live their life fully. You can still hold your love for that person and the memory, but cords between the living and dead don't serve either party. For the living, a strong energetic cord can even create a feeling of being pulled toward death. The survivor may not feel suicidal and may feel that they have many things to live for, but still be drawn to and fascinated with death. This may manifest itself as an illness, emotional issues, or a loss of enthusiasm for life.

The first step in cord cutting is to be clear about which cords you want to cut. You need to decide if you want to cut all cords except to your higher self, if you want to keep the pure love cords that bind you to loved ones, and if you want to keep cords to happy memories or just the memories. Also, decide if you want to cut cords in a general way — all the ones that meet your criteria — or specific cords. Sometimes cords need to be cut individually, with focused intent, or they reattach later. For example, if you and your lover of ten years have parted ways, you will definitely want to cut those cords individually, possibly several times and in several ways. For cords that have a great deal of emotion behind them, it requires a more focused intention to effectively cut them, whereas random cords created as you were driving down the freeway or daydreaming can be cut in mass.

There are a number of different approaches you can take to cutting cords. One of the simplest is to visualize severing cords that you do not wish to carry. You can picture scissors, a knife, a sword, or an athame. Just make sure you set your intent so that your tool is much bigger and sharper than anything it might need to cut through. This visualization is a good one to use in the moment when you're aware of cords. For example, if someone is rude to you at the post office and it gets under your skin, cut the cord. It can also be used at night before you go to bed to cut away all the cords you may have picked up during the day. The visualization can be as vivid and detailed or as general as you choose.

Another technique for cutting cords is to ask your angels, guides, and/or helpers to come in and cut the cords you want to sever. Be sure to be very specific in your intent when making this request. This is a very simple way to cut cords; however, if you have a cord that you haven't processed all the way, it may reattach shortly there after. Your spirit helpers are excellent at removing cords that other people have sent to you.

Many indigenous cultures deal with the concept of cord cutting. The Hawaiians use a technique called Ho'o pono pono to sever what they refer to as aka cords. Likewise, Incan shamanic practices include cord cutting.

I prefer to cut cords within a shamanic journey. The work seems to go deeper because I am accessing both the conscious and unconscious parts of myself. In a journey to cut cords, I go to my sacred garden with a clear intent about which cords I want to cut. Once I cross into shamanic reality, I can perceive the cords that connect to my physical and energetic body by asking to see them. When cutting cords in shamanic reality, use your tool of choice—a sword, golden scissors, etc.—and cut through the cords you have selected to remove. You may see the cords falling away to ashes after they are cut or they may simply disappear.

After you have cut the cords away, you can do some healing work on the area where the cord was attached. Sometimes major cords can do damage to the auric field, leaving it more vulnerable to future cord attachment. You can heal the area by visualizing white light or energy pouring into it and darkness, pain, or damage rushing out. Or you can ask your guides to provide a healing for you.

Whatever approach you choose, cutting cords is a way to free up life force energy. It is a means of releasing past traumas, letting go of finished relationships, and setting up good energetic boundaries. Cutting cords can even free us from past life wounds. Furthermore, the fewer energetic cords you have, the more consciously you can control your mood, thoughts, and state of being. By reducing the number of energies flowing randomly into and out of your energetic field, you are better able to center yourself and set your own energy.

Ancestors

Many cultures honor or even worship their ancestors. It's not so much that these practices make the ancestors happy, but that they remind the descendents of all the strength and wisdom and ability to deal with a changing world that is their legacy. Thinking about our ancestors in these terms connects us to the support and help they offer us. When asked for support, our ancestors will line up, with our mother's line behind one shoulder and our father's line behind the other, offering strength, wisdom, and unconditional love. Their energies flow down the ancestral line to us and to our children.

Our ancestors watch over and protect us as we grow. They can be like spirit guides, teachers, or guardian angels. When we speak of ancestors, we refer to people who have died to whom we have a familial connection, be it through blood, adoption, or family of choice. In fact, adopted children may call upon double the ancestral support—that of their biological line as well as that of their adopted line. Sometimes we also have spiritual ancestors, people who mastered life lessons and energies that we are working with in our lifetimes. A spiritual ancestor might be an ascended master or teacher, an elder in our spiritual heritage, or the founder of a martial art we study, for example.

Our ancestors will support us to the best of their ability, unconditionally. However, sometimes there is healing that was incomplete for them in their lifetime. It may be that a relationship needs healing or it may be personal healing. In those cases, they may look to their descendents for help. When things are out of alignment in our family lines, the flow of energy is blocked and stymied from one generation to the next. The more healed and whole our ancestors are, the more easily and fully the love will flow. It is a beautiful full circle to do healing work with your ancestors, to hold them with compassion, and to align your family energy. The personal benefits are great, but there is no obligation when opportunities arise to do healing work with your ancestors. My ancestors make it very clear that they stand behind me and hold me, not the other way around.

Sometimes a call for help from an ancestor can manifest as a physical symptom. If a father died of a heart attack at age fifty, his son or daughter may begin to experience heart pain at that age, despite a healthy heart. Sometimes when you show up to help an ancestor because of a physical symptom, they will open the door for more extensive family healing. For example, my great-great-grandmother had throat cancer and died shortly after I was born. I was experiencing chronic energy blocks in my throat chakra, so I went to offer healing to her in case there was a connection.

When I met her, she let me know that while she wouldn't object to some healing, what she truly desired was my help for her daughter, my great-grandmother. The work I did provided healing for my maternal line and resolved the problems with my throat chakra. Afterwards we all gathered in the garden of the house they had lived in: my great-great grandmother, my great-grandmother, and my beloved grandmother. I felt how intensely they loved me and how proud they were of me.

When a family pattern is healed by doing healing work with an ancestor, not only does it affect them, it also provides a healing for everyone in that line, forward and backward. For example, say there is a theme of mothers not connecting fully with their daughters that has been handed down for generations. You can go to the source of that problem or the most recent example of that problem and do healing work. Either way, that healing will be reflected through the maternal line, especially impacting all the living descendents.

Shamanic journeying can also be used to better understand the gifts of our family legacies. You can journey to your ancestors and ask them to show you what gifts come from your family line. Do this journey for the maternal side, the paternal side, and your spiritual ancestors as separate journeys. My father's side offers an intense connection to the land and the ability to hold myself in place, easily, no matter what's happening in the world around me. My ancestors showed me this by having me stand in a huge river to show me I wouldn't be swept away. On my mother's side, one of the gifts is connection to others, the ability to form a light web of mutual support. One spiritual ancestor showed me how to shapechange into animals in shamanic reality.

Ancestors also have valuable information for us about our own families and family dynamics. It can be immensely helpful for us in having compassion for our parents if we understand what their parents struggled with. For example, part of my grandmother saw herself as monstrous and knowing this allowed me to understand the strange disowned shadows that energy cast between her and my mother and my mother and myself.

Healing work with ancestors can happen in a couple of ways. One is if you have a specific issue you want to heal, physical or emotional. You might ask for help with the pain in your foot and be taken to a several times great-grandparent who had their foot amputated. You might have a specific family issue that you want to heal, like a theme of physical violence or constant criticism. Or you may specifically ask to do ancestral healing work and ask that you be taken to an ancestor in need of healing. Whichever you pick, set your intent clearly, go to your garden, and ask your guides to help you.

When you find yourself with the ancestor in need of healing, watch and listen or ask your guide what you can do to help. Perhaps your ancestor simply needs to tell their story. It may be appropriate to call in light beings or angels to heal them. It may be good to send them energy directly. Whatever the case, there are a couple of guidelines to be aware of:

Don't ask to do any work with someone who has died in the last year; they need time to adjust to the absence of a physical body. If they come to you sooner in shamanic reality, that's fine, but don't seek them out.

As with anyone, an ancestor is free to accept or reject any healing you may offer them. If they reject healing, you do not have the right to force the issue. At the same time, you have the right to decline the legacy of that unhealed issue. If your ancestor declines your help for healing, you can ask your guides to show you how to heal the issue for yourself and your line and you can cut the energetic cords tying you to that issue.

One of my ancestors died young, leaving her toddler son behind. When I approached her in shamanic reality, she was pacing back and forth, back and forth, oblivious to me, even when I spoke to her and tried to get her attention. So I asked that some healing energy go into her environment if she didn't object. She didn't, and when the energy began to build around her, she stopped pacing and noticed me for the first time. The son had experienced soul loss as a result of her death, so a part of him was adrift. I brought that part to his mother and they were joyfully reunited. I let them hang out for a while and then asked the boy if he wanted to return to the grandparent he'd be separated from and the mother if she'd like my help to move on.

They both said "no" very emphatically. They were overjoyed at being reunited and not ready to move forward. A few years later, I did another journey back to check on them. At that point, the boy indicated that he'd be interested in going back to my grandfather and my great-grandmother said that if he went back, she'd be willing to move on. Of the power animals that help me with soul retrieval, the hawk is the one that retrieves and delivers soul parts. The boy left riding my hawk. My great-grandmother and I had a cup of tea while we waited and when my hawk came back saying the soul part that was the boy had been returned, she moved on with three of her female relatives who came in to guide her.

Our ancestors offer many gifts—love, support, a better understanding of who we are and where we came from. The more consciously you connect to your ancestors, through traditional means or through shamanic work, the more you open yourself to the gifts that they bring.

Past life work

Steve Rother says that if you want to see a past life, you need look no further than your garage. It is a useful metaphor because it points to the human tendency to hold onto things that have outlived their usefulness. We keep them because we think we might one day need them or because we can't bear to part with the reminder of a past experience. But all of these things fill up the space in our lives until we can't move freely or find the things we need in the present.

This practice of holding onto things that no longer serve us, be they physical or energetic, saps our vitality. We are capable of tying up huge amounts of the space in our lives with things of the past that don't contribute to the present from this lifetime alone. The last thing we want to do is add past life clutter. So, when I apply shamanism to past life work, it is generally for the purpose of cleaning spiritual house and getting rid of all the old energy from past lives that adversely affect the present.

Sadly, some people's primary exposure to those who believe in past lives is to those few who make extravagant claims of having been a spectacular or even historical figure. Trust me, even the staunchest believers in reincarnation question the truth of those sorts of claims and, even more so, the motives of the people bringing it up. Most of the people who believe in reincarnation don't believe they were the high priest of the Druids or a princess in Egypt. And the people who really were aren't advertising it.

So, must you believe in past lives to gain benefit from this kind of shamanic work? Absolutely not. In general, where past lives are concerned, most people have the veil firmly in place, preventing them from knowing about other lives they lived. And rightly so: there is plenty to work on in this life without devoting significant attention to past lives. Furthermore, I believe that any issue or lessons that we are working to resolve from a past lifetime will be activated through the events and experiences in this lifetime.

Past lives can be viewed as stories that resonate for people with different intensities. For some people it is a fundamental truth of their existence; for others there is a hint and a whisper that they might have experienced something before; for others, there is absolutely no sense of having lived before. It may sound counterintuitive but, when I direct my attention to past lives, it is for the purpose of freeing up my energy to be fully in this lifetime.

To begin this work, I recommend you journey to your garden with the intent to seek your guides' assistance for any past life issues in need of healing. This may be a general kind of thing or it may involve some very specific questions. Some cues that a past life healing may be in order include things like a powerful fear that you can't explain. For example, if you are terrified of heights, but have never had a bad experience, the fear might reflect falling and injuring yourself in a previous life. A very intense negative reaction to a person, place, or thing can be another indication of a past life issue. Or a pattern that feels like it's been repeated over and over again may go back further than you think.

You can always ask your guides, "Does this issue primarily come from a past life experience?" You can also ask general questions, such as, "What needs healing as regards to how I connect with men?" "Why am I having such a strong reaction to this person, place, thing, idea?" "What is the source of my fear about relationships, work, dark places?" The answer may be related to a past life or it may be something else. Your guides will be able to tell or show you the answer.

One of the more memorable personal experiences I've had with past life work related to a man I was very attracted to. Despite having reached my late twenties, it felt very much like a teenage crush, with all the drama, hope, and anxiety—very far from my usual style. At the time it also brought up intense insecurities—I was too fat, too shy, not attractive enough, and so on. Naturally, I wasn't especially thrilled with all this stuff being dragged up, but I chose to look at it as an opportunity to heal.

In a shamanic state, I was shown a past life connection to this person. I was standing on the deck of a ship, bound for the new world and a new life. I was eager to make a life there. As I stood on the deck of this ship, he approached and I looked up and smiled. He walked past me without even seeing me, his attention riveted on a delicate, feminine woman. In that moment, I first felt inadequate. Up to then, I had felt strong and sure of myself. I was hearty and hardworking, everything I should be as a woman in a culture that shunned physical vanity. At that moment, when I first felt this inadequacy, my good and healthy esteem for my own strengths shifted into a shield to protect me against being judged unworthy by this new, previously unconsidered standard.

This past life information gave me the freedom to make my intelligence and independence less rigid and less protective, allowing me to express more of my sexual girl energy. And the man? It turned out we were woefully ill-suited, but for the initial moments of our time together he looked at me as if I were the most beautiful, fascinating woman he had ever seen. In the absence of past life work, it would still have been a healing experience to have his brief admiration. But with the past life work, the healing went far deeper. Without the conscious understanding of where my insecurity about my attractiveness to men originated, I suspect I would have spent a good deal more time coming to understand that lesson.

Your guides will come up with custom tailored ways to heal past life issues. But I want to share a few of the techniques my guides have used with me.

One of the simplest means of healing a past life issue does not involve an exploration of the details of a past life, but merely the intent to sever ties or cords to that life. While there is sometimes pain with healing, it's not always a requirement. In my opinion, where past life work is concerned, it's best if the work isn't emotional or heart-wrenching. While we may feel resonances for the people we were, the experiences we've had, or the people we knew, it's still important to keep good, clear boundaries regarding the fact that this is not our current lifetime. The idea is to release the pain and wounds from other lifetimes, not to relive them or process them.

Processing all the bad things that happened to us in other lifetimes takes away too much time and energy from living this lifetime. Humans throughout the ages have not always played well together and the absence of modern medicine often made for early and grim deaths, so there's a lot to say for not going there in detail if possible. To cut cords or ties to other lives, ask your guides to show them to you. Then use one of the techniques discussed in the section on cutting cords to sever them.

Much as I like the cord-cutting approach, sometimes there is value in seeing the details of a situation. For example, in the experience I related, there was a great deal of value in being able to see how I used my areas of strength and security as a shield against the feelings of vulnerability that arose around my more feminine aspects. Releasing the energy from that life was one level of healing, but understanding the complex pattern that grew from that moment provided a whole other level of healing. Your guides should be able to help you strike a balance between seeing the details and simply cutting the cords.

One good rule of thumb for deciding whether you want to explore the details of a past life experience is looking at what the issue relates to. If it is something that relates to your physical safety and well-being in a fundamental way, you will probably do well simply to cut the cords rather than look at images of your past self dying messily or being harmed in some way. On the other hand, if it relates to your relationships to others or how you see yourself, a more detailed exploration may prove useful.

The other possibility is simply to start with the cord cutting method and see whether that resolves things. If it does, great. If not, try delving deeper. In a situation where you feel the need to see the details, it is likely that this theme has appeared in more than one lifetime. You can look at the most recent time it occurred or the first time it occurred or both. The middle times it happened seem to be less relevant.

Past life work can provide a powerful form of healing. It's just important to remember that the goal is to free up energy to be fully and completely in this lifetime and, in fact, in the now. Shamanic journeying can even be used to explore who you were and what other lives were like, rather than to resolve issues. It can be fascinating and informative, but remember, it's okay to look back, as long as you don't stare.

Contracts and oaths

Alberto Villoldo tells a story of a woman who came to him after learning that her adult daughter had been diagnosed with breast cancer. On his shamanic journey, Villoldo saw a scene that seemed to be from a past life play out. She and her children were trapped beneath a collapsed house, slowly freezing to death. As she held her dying children, the woman prayed that her children would die before her so that she could hold them and comfort them as they died. Unfortunately, the universe didn't register that the prayer was only for that one situation. The passion and intensity of her request created an energetic tendency to ensure those circumstances in other lifetimes. Villoldo renegotiated that request on her behalf to "Make sure my children always know that I love them."

The contracts we set up and the oaths we swear in this lifetime and others have a huge impact on our lives. Our intentions define how we interact with world. In the physical world, our choices inform our actions, which afford us various outcomes. In the shamanic and energetic world, our intention shapes our relationship and what we receive from the universe. So, whenever we make a vow, promise, or oath with the full weight of our passion and intention behind it, be it to ourselves or to someone else, the universe takes us at our word and supports us in manifesting that oath.

When it comes to contracts, oaths, and promises, there are three types in play. The first is the oaths that we swear this lifetime. Then there are the promises and vows from other lifetimes. Finally there are the soul contracts that we set up prior to taking on our physical bodies.

With the oaths from this lifetime, it might be a commitment to yourself to eat better or a promise to love someone 'till death do you part." The oaths from this lifetime include the promises we make to ourselves in childhood about never being vulnerable or never trusting again. These oaths and vows are the easiest to work with because we have all the information. Even if we don't consciously remember the childhood oaths, conventional forms of therapy allow us to reason our way back to those intentions based on what we know about our childhood and our patterns today.

The contracts, oaths, and promises from past lives, such as the one discussed in the beginning of this section, are somewhat more complicated. One of the most common oaths from a past life is the intent never to use your spiritual gifts again. A cursory glance at history will show that people who had abilities that their neighbors didn't understand were likely to experience rejection at best and violent death at worst. In a world that burned people at the stake as witches, a person with spiritual abilities would become very invested in disowning, denying, and suppressing those abilities. Any time we made a vow in another lifetime with great passion and intention, it had the potential to create an energetic stamp that carried into the next lifetime.

Finally, there are the contracts and plans we set up for ourselves before incarnating. For many people, the idea that we plan our life while we are in spirit form has great resonance. According to this philosophy, we pick our families and our life path. We choose lessons that we want to work on and select gifts to explore different passions. When we incarnate, we don't have a conscious memory of the life lessons and passions we have selected to explore. But there is great universal support and impetus toward those things, starting with the family we are born into.

When we feel a soul yearning to do or be something, it points to those contracts and plans. When people talk about finding your passion and living your passion, from a shamanic perspective they are talking about being in alignment with the soul contracts you picked for yourself. It could be having children, a creative expression such as art or music, a healing path, engineering, science—whatever makes your heart sing.

The overachievers among us may have a number of contracts and lessons they are working on.

When we move down a path that is in alignment with those soul contracts, there is a great deal of support and help coming from the universe. In fact, the world around us will keep giving us opportunities and encouragement. These opportunities may be in the form of things that we experiences as negative, such as illness or hardship that promotes a life lesson. Or they may be in a more enjoyable form, in which we meet the right people and have the opportunity to move into our passion.

Given that contracts, oaths, and promises communicate to the universe what opportunities and experiences we want it to manifest in our lives, I advocate choosing your promises with great care. In and of themselves, contracts, oaths, and commitments are neither good nor bad; they simply inform the universe what to send our way. In other words, a contract or an oath is a means of focusing intention to manifest a given situation or experience while our conscious attention is occupied elsewhere.

For example, let's say you decide before you incarnate that you want to have a daughter and set up a contract with another soul to be her mother. Let's say that you also plan that you want to have your child in your mid-thirties in order to give yourself time to work on other lessons first. The soul contract would direct the universe to give you opportunities to learn certain lessons before your thirties and to set up circumstances that would support having a child at that age. Children might be the furthest thing from your mind right up until you reach your mid-thirties, but the universe would still be working in the background to make sure you have the opportunity.

With any oaths and contracts, be they from this lifetime, a previous lifetime, or a soul contract, we have free choice. We have the option to choose not to keep a given contract or to renegotiate it. Going back to the example of the daughter, if you decide you don't want to be a parent, that's perfectly okay, and there are often back-up plans for that soul to be born to someone else and to come into your life as a neighbor's child or a student.

The idea that we should always keep our word is a vast oversimplification of a good principle. Keeping our word blindly allows us to get locked into situations that don't serve us or those around us, such as staying in a bad relationship because we made a commitment. When it comes to promises, a better principle is to take responsibility for our word. We have the right to choose and if we find that a choice no longer fits, we have the right to choose again.

In the physical world, with the active promises we've made to ourselves and others, we have the right to renegotiate. There isn't a simple rule for right and wrong when it comes to renegotiating promises to others. Some are straightforward. If you promised to pick a friend up at the airport but your mother needs you to drive her to the hospital for an emergency, it's clearly appropriate to renegotiate with your friend. Others, like a professional agreement that has become inconvenient to fulfill, may require a great deal more thought and creativity to find a solution that honors the rights and well-being of both people.

If you can't come up with a new arrangement in any situation that is a win-win, choosing not to fulfill a promise may be the best option for you, but it may also cost you the trust and esteem of the other person. How to handle contracts and promises isn't the easiest question, but it's familiar territory. We have a body of law and collective sense of right and wrong that deal with promises between people. The better a job you do of taking responsibly for your commitments and making sure both your needs and the other party's are met, the better your relationship will be to the people around you.

In the energetic and shamanic world, you also have the right to renegotiate contracts. There's an observation that no battle plan survives contact with the enemy. Likewise, the soul contracts that seem perfect and wonderful before incarnating may not be as good a fit as we begin to actually live our lives. People have free choice and the ways we impact each other's lives can be unpredictable. As your life unfolds, if you decide that you wish to follow a different path than the one you picked before you were born, that choice is honored, without judgment.

Alberto Villoldo talks about a practice called Destiny Retrieval in which shamanic techniques are used to select a different life path than the one you're on. For example, let's say someone is dying from a terminal illness and that they have completed all the work and lessons that they planned on when they incarnated. They may have planned to die at a given time, but then decide that they really would like to explore some other things. They might choose a new life path with new soul contracts—consciously or unconsciously— survive the illness and go down a completely different path.

Shamanic tools can be immensely helpful in ensuring that all your contracts and oaths serve you well. First and foremost, you can use shamanic journeying to understand the oaths, contracts, and promises you have made on an energetic level and which ones are having the strongest impact on the circumstances that are manifesting in your life. To do this, go to your place of power and ask your guides whichever of the following questions feel like the best fit:

- What are the primary contracts from past lives that are impacting this lifetime?

- Please show me any contracts that are taking me out of right relationship to the universe.

- What are my soul contracts that are in play at this moment?

- What choices am I making in my life that are out of alignment with my soul contracts?

- How has my life today diverged from my plan for my lifetime?

- What oaths did I swear as a child that are impacting my life today?

- What am I unconsciously asking the universe to manifest on my behalf?

- Is this issue the result of a contract or oath?

Once you have gathered information about the nature of your contracts and oaths, you can begin to act on them. If you have a vow from a past life never to use your healing abilities again, you may want to renounce that oath. If your promise to stay with someone forever is not serving either of you, you may want to reconsider that contract. If you have a soul contract to heal through music, you may want to consciously engage with that contract by taking singing lessons or learning to play an instrument. Larger soul contracts may take a great deal of soul-searching and consideration before you decide to fulfill them or renegotiate them. Again, you can do a journey with the intent to seek the assistance and input of your guides on any of the following questions or intents:

- Please help me to renegotiate this contract from a past life.

- What would be the outcome of fulfilling this soul contract?

- What would be the outcome of choosing not to fulfill this soul contract?

- Please help me explore the question of whether this plan or promise still fits for me.

- What steps can I take right now to open the door to this soul contract?

Contracts, oaths, and promises are very powerful on an energetic level. Even people who don't have any interest in spirituality or metaphysics are likely to understand the importance and significance of keeping a promise. In many of our myths and stories, the plot hinges around the character's choice to honor or not honor a promise when the ramifications far exceed anything they could have predicted. In short, the concept of promises and oaths has enormous weight and resonance within the human experience.

As you move through the world, make sure your oaths, promises, and contracts are working for you and not against you. Honor the contracts by taking the time to explore them and renegotiate them, but do not be bound by them or let them prevent you from choosing again when that is needed. For the promises that serve you well, let the oath and contract help to manifest and support that outcome as you consciously work toward a given goal. When you spend your energy in a manner that is in alignment with a contract, help will come from all directions and a small effort will bring a great result.

Chapter 11—Getting All the Pieces Back: Shadow Work and Soul Retrieval

Shadow work

As human beings, we have many sides and aspects. The parts of myself that come out to play with friends are often different from those parts that are expressed at work. My sexual nature is a great example of this—as much as I embrace that aspect of my being, I don't express it with co-workers or clients. There are aspects of our conscious, waking selves as well as more elusive, intuitive aspects that come from deeper, less conscious levels of being. Every part offers gifts and resources as we move through life. The challenge is to get all these aspects working harmoniously so that we apply the most helpful aspect for each situation.

Unfortunately, we generally grow up learning that certain aspects of ourselves are "bad" and "wrong," rather than receiving guidance in how to apply them correctly. In fact, we find our families and school systems working both covertly and overtly to prevent us from standing up for ourselves. Parents and teachers frequently find it much easier to deal with children who obey, keep quiet, and don't express painful emotions.

Over time, we may develop an adversarial relationship with ourselves, sorting aspects of ourselves into categories of "good" and "bad." Our self-esteem becomes dependent on how effectively we can disown certain aspects of ourselves. These aspects become what is generally referred to in the metaphysical community as our shadows. Our shadows include all the things about ourselves that we are ashamed of and wish would go away. They can be made of many things: emotions that we have polarized as "bad," such as anger or sadness; traits and qualities that we have been made to feel ashamed of; or aspects of our sexuality.

To identify your shadow, look at what you judge most harshly in others, what qualities or behaviors produce a disproportionately negative reaction. We frequently condemn our disowned shadows in others. Perhaps you can't stand loud people or sloppy people or those who are overweight. Even if you don't embody the quality and have effectively suppressed it in yourself, if you get very upset with people who express that aspect, it is an indicator of your disowned shadow. Ironically, the more we try to hide, suppress, and control these shadow aspects, the more likely they are to pop up at the worst possible time and in the most inappropriate manner, reinforcing the desire to disown them. This process ties up a huge amount of vitality and life energy and leaves us feeling fragmented and in conflict with ourselves.

In some cases, disowning an aspect can lead to soul loss. Instead of becoming an aspect that is disowned and disenfranchised, but still a part of you, the part actually leaves, becoming separate and taking away part of your life energy. This often happens when a child feels that an aspect cannot, must not be a part of them if they are to survive—physically or emotionally. So they send it away. A way to determine whether a shadow part has actually left completely is if there is a complete absence of an aspect that everyone else seems to have. You can also do a shamanic journey to ask your guides if you have experienced soul loss due to disowned aspects. Healing this kind of experience calls for a soul retrieval, which I discuss in a later section. But more often, we simply strive to ignore and suppress these aspects of ourselves, rather than sending them away.

When it comes to shadow work, lightworkers often shy away, or approach it like the energetic equivalent of nasty tasting medicine that will improve spiritual health. And yet, as I write on the topic, I am reminded of Peter Pan, weeping because he's lost his shadow and cannot get it reattached. After Wendy sews it back on, he is once more filled with joy and light and the magic of flight. To carry the analogy a bit further, it was a bit uncomfortable when Wendy sewed the shadow back on, but it was the loss of it, not the pricking, that made Peter cry.

Often we feel that our shadow aspects are big and terrible and unlovable, so it's no wonder that even when we have resolved to do work on integrating our shadow aspects, we feel trepidation. Yet, when it comes to shadow work, it's been my experience that what seems huge and terrible and frightening is much smaller and much more appealing when looked at differently. Picture the shadow of a huge, terrifying monster that turns out to be cast by a kitten moving around under a blanket.

The gifts of this work are huge. When you reclaim and reintegrate these disowned aspects, you increase your vitality and life energy. Reintegrated shadow parts invariably improve our sense of wholeness, protecting and strengthening us, allowing us to be more spontaneous and present in daily life.

We also deny our strengths and potentials, separating ourselves from the ability to realize our lives as we desire them to be. In this case, these aspects are often things that you admire passionately in others. For example, say you deeply admire the Dalai Lama. When you look at that more closely, you might realize that the admiration is primarily for his ability to stay centered in difficult situations or his ability to combine laughter and spirituality. His power and influence may not matter or may be at the core of what you respond to. Whatever the specific quality, what you most appreciate is the fully realized aspect of some potential within yourself.

When we look at qualities and aspects of ourselves as binary, that is, present or absent, we talk ourselves out of even trying to develop the absent parts. For any given talent or attribute, there will always be people better at it and worse at it, so comparisons are meaningless. Effort and attention are required to develop a potential quality and it's fine to choose consciously not to invest that effort. It is unfortunate that many people don't make this sort of choice consciously. When we say we admire something in someone else and that we could never be that thing, we deny a part of ourselves and give ourselves permission not to grow or strive, without even owning that choice.

A shamanic journey is an excellent way to understand and reclaim our disowned aspects. By dealing with them nonverbally through symbols, myths, and archetypes, we can understand these parts in a manner that would be hard to grasp in our day-to-day experience. While our conscious experience may offer insight and awareness of what aspects we've disowned, shamanic work is a tool for the full reintegration of those aspects. Furthermore, when using shamanic methods to do this work, you can take along extra help and support in the form of spirit guides and power animals.

The first time I journeyed to do shadow work, a group of spirit guides helped me to prepare ritually for this work by dancing around me and painting my face before they led me to a cave to meet my shadow aspect. As I went on alone, downward into the dark, toward the light of a fire, I knew I carried the power and support of my guides. Myths and stories of the journey into the unknown have always resonated very strongly for me. So, when my guides framed the experience as a type of heroic journey, it gave me a context for my fear and apprehension and allowed me to go forward despite these feelings.

When I found my shadow aspects waiting for me in my sacred garden, I had the opportunity to interact with that part of myself as though it was a separate being. My disowned shadow looked exactly as I had projected it to be—ugly and scary. In addition, it was angry and hurt. It had come as a part of me with nothing but gifts and good intentions to support me in the world and I had categorically rejected it, leaving it unloved and unacknowledged. This aspect of myself was carrying some of my childhood wounds and insecurities.

But, when I got past my own fear and saw things from this other point of view, my shadow self had a great deal to tell me. When I stopped projecting onto this aspect, I saw a little girl, not scary at all. My shadow aspects had bound up a lot of my strength, resilience, and ability to protect myself. When I reintegrated all aspects of these characteristics, I suddenly had access to my inherent strength and power. It was not an easy journey, but one of the most rewarding.

If you decide to do a shamanic journey to explore aspects of yourself you've disowned, pick a time when you're feeling especially secure and centered. Be very aware that the journey may be emotionally challenging and that if gets to be too much, you have the option to stop. As I've mentioned before, I don't believe in spiritual masochism or machismo, especially with shadow work. If you are overwhelmingly afraid, you can do more harm than good.

If shadow work feels especially scary, I recommend you start with a separate journey to gather resources and obtain healing before you actually meet with your shadow aspect. Ask your guides for help and suggestions for how this work can be both powerful and gentle. Perhaps they will offer to hold your hand or sit beside you. They might offer healing and help you work through some of the childhood wounds that led to the disowning of a given part. Perhaps they will suggest some things you could do in your waking life, such as journaling, to start exploring aspects you have disowned before you meet them in shamanic reality.

When meeting with your disowned aspects, you have the chance to talk to them and hear their point of view. There is the opportunity to understand what caused you to reject these parts of yourself. You can ask what gifts each aspect will bring into your life and how you can make it feel welcome. As you come to a place to reintegrate it, it is literally an experience of getting back a piece of yourself. All the internal conflict of rejecting a part of yourself falls away and the energy of that conflict can be redirected to goals of your choosing. Your sense and value of yourself become more solid and complete. Shadow work, the experience of accepting and acknowledging every part of ourselves without labeling it "good" or "bad," is a fundamental part of becoming whole.

Soul retrieval

Soul retrieval is dear to my heart. It is one of the gentlest, most graceful and profound healing practices. My own soul retrieval was life changing and I always feel a special joy when a client picks a soul retrieval from among my healing services.

The term "soul retrieval" can be confusing. While the term "soul" is often used, it is difficult to define. In soul retrieval, the soul is the energetic essence of your being. It encompasses the intangible aspects of your being, including gifts, qualities, and aspects of who you are. The soul in soul retrieval is our spiritual being and essence. The existential question of the nature of the soul isn't important for the practice of soul retrieval, aside from the concept that the spiritual or life essence that composes your soul can become fragmented. In other words, pieces and parts of that soul essence can become separated, trapped, and lost. If you imagine the soul energy as a sphere, when soul loss occurs, there are voids and areas that are missing.

Soul loss is part of the human experience. It's designed to protect our nonphysical essence from various kinds of trauma. If something traumatic is happening such as a car accident, physical violence, or an emotional assault, the last place we want to be is fully present in our bodies and in the experience. Instead, part of us goes away to avoid the trauma. Psychologists refer to this as dissociation. The shamanic community calls it soul loss. Either way, it helps us to survive the various kinds of trauma that happen in our lives.

There are lots of kinds of trauma that can cause soul loss. Anything that happened to you that caused you physical injury or really got your adrenaline flowing has the potential to cause soul loss—for example, accidents, surgery, sexual violence, or combat trauma. Whenever someone says, "I've never been the same since my accident, that relationship, my surgery," they are describing a soul loss experience. Trauma that causes soul loss can be subtle and different for each person. Being teased or shamed can cause a sensitive child to lose soul parts. Sandra Ingerman tells the story of a client who experienced soul loss at the age of three when her mother wouldn't let her climb a tree.

Whatever the trauma, the protective mechanism of soul loss causes part of our life essence to leave in order to protect itself from being damaged or traumatized. The soul part leaving sometimes carries away some of the memory and immediacy of the experience. In the normal course of events, the soul essence would return on its own after the trauma had passed. But sometimes the trauma is so severe that the soul part goes so far and fast that it can't find its way back and gets lost. In cases of chronic trauma or abuse, the soul part may not know it's safe to come back. There's no time in shamanic reality, so the soul part doesn't know that twenty years have passed and the violent stepfather is no longer in the picture.

Another type of soul loss is when a part leaves because it doesn't fit or because it is sent away. This could be an aspect that is shamed or punished; for example, a girl might send away her anger. Any quality that is likely to be disruptive to an already dysfunctional family is likely to be sent away by a child because further destabilization of the family endangers their survival and well-being. I've also seen people lose parts to disillusionment, often in their twenties. There was no trauma, but some part of themselves wasn't finding expression and left.

Finally, soul loss can happen when parts of our soul are taken by or given to the significant people in our lives. A child's mother may take the part that her mother took from her and her mother before her and so on. As human beings, we struggle to maintain good physical and emotional boundaries. The concept of good energetic boundaries is not something that occurs to most people. When soul parts are taken or exchanged, it invariably happens on an unconscious, energetic level. People who have had soul parts taken unknowingly take soul parts from others. While there's no judgment or blame, this does put people in an inappropriate energetic relationship.

Picture a mother, already diminished by her own soul loss experiences, looking at her child. She might think that if she could just have some of her child's vitality and energy, she would be able to cope with her life. On an energetic level, she reaches out and takes some of the child's essence. The child may resist at first, but eventually it is easier to give up the soul part than keep struggling. Or perhaps the child feels sorry for the parent and gives up their soul part willingly. Again, I want to emphasize that this isn't deliberate. When I retrieve soul parts, parents are always glad to give up their children's soul parts once they realize what they've done.

In a romantic relationship, the people involved often will trade soul parts. Our culture's love mythology implies that when we love someone, we give them our heart and our soul. It's easy to mistake a lack of energetic boundaries for closeness and connection. People often unconsciously give their lover some of their own vital life essence along with their love. This exchange makes both people more dependent on each other, less able to stand on their own, and thus less likely to leave. It can feel safer and more connected to both parties, but in reality, both people are diminished.

Whatever the source of soul loss, the effects are much the same. Soul loss will diminish a person's sense of well-being and joy in life. It can cause a lack of vitality and interest in the world. People often feel depressed, listless, and as though the world was all gray. Soul loss can lead to gaps in memory. People can feel fragmented or spacey or even like pieces are missing. People with soul loss can spend a lot of energy working through events of their past and still feel impacted by them. In extreme cases, soul loss can cause a lack of sense of self, suicidal tendencies, and vulnerability to physical illness.

When someone comes to me for a soul retrieval I talk to them about the potential impact on their lives, because a soul retrieval can be life-altering. It's a powerfully healing, but afterwards my client may find it much harder to accept situations where they are not being honored, regardless of the economic or emotional advantages of being in that place. The universe will support and take care of us in the transitions we make. But change is uncomfortable and the faster growth happens, the more unsettled life will be.

This is particularly true if someone has given soul parts to another person. In some cases, returning the soul parts to my client places them instantly in a more appropriate relationship to the people in their lives who had previously held their soul parts. Tensions and conflict may dissipate overnight without the other parties even being aware that a soul retrieval took place. In other cases, if a marriage is teetering on the edge, for example, a soul retrieval could be the end of it. Any relationship where the other person is invested in controlling my client is likely to be made rockier by a soul retrieval. This is because a soul retrieval makes the recipient stronger, more complete, and harder to control.

On the other hand, for people who have left a major relationship and are finding that they are having trouble moving on, a soul retrieval may be the perfect thing. Very often a soul part is left behind with the former spouse or lover and returning that to my client frees them to move on.

When I do a soul retrieval for someone, my guides have told me to start out by standing in a waterfall to make sure I am completely energetically clear before I begin. Then I build a fire in my sacred garden and dance around it until my soul retrieval spirit guides arrive. We then go forth together to Lower World to retrieve power animals that will support my client through the reintegration process. After meeting my client's power animals, I ask their spirit guides if there is a message or information for my client.

At that point, the true soul retrieval work begins. I step into a shamanic void and wait for the soul pieces I will be bringing back to light up, showing me how many there are and where they are located. My horse then carries me to each of them in the order that my guides agree is most appropriate. They seldom select a chronological order. At that point I work with the soul parts in whatever situation I find them.

If the soul part is alone, I talk to it about how my client is ready to receive it back and would like it to return. I give it space to tell me its story. Sometimes the part talks to me about why it left, sometimes not. I note the surroundings in which I find the soul part and how old it appears to be. If the soul part is a child soul part, it will often insist that it wants to ride on my horse with me, whereas older soul parts are often content to return as energy. Together we go forth to find the next soul part.

If the soul part is a part that is held by someone else in my client's life, I negotiate for that person to voluntarily release it. Before I even make that request, I offer a soul retrieval for the person holding my client's soul part. My hawk will go forth and bring back the soul parts that this person lost that caused them to take the soul part from my client. It's not a complete soul retrieval, but invariably after the shamanic aspect of that person has their own soul part returned, they are willing to relinquish my client's. In shamanic reality, the person holding my client's soul part has better access to their higher self. So however disconnected from their love and compassion they may be in ordinary reality, they often experience those emotions in the shamanic world.

As I mentioned, when you get a soul part back from another person, there is often an impact on the relationship. For an adult, getting their childhood soul parts back from their parents can smooth out the energetic relationship. The return of a soul part from a former lover or spouse can free you to move forward. If someone who held your soul part has died, returning that soul part has a powerful benefit for both of you. It frees the soul of the other person to move on, unburdened by energy that they can't use. But for my client, it can release them from a fascination with and a pull toward death. It's not a common situation, but sometimes when a loved one dies without relinquishing a major soul part, there can be an energetic pull for that person to die before their time.

Once I've gathered up the three to six soul pieces that my guides have identified as the most critical, I stand on a cliff and cast an energetic net into the person's past lives. I pull forward any soul energy that was left behind or trapped there and add it to the other parts I am bringing back. For some clients, there is a huge amount of life essence from past lives, for other only a small bit.

Once I have gathered all the soul parts and energy, I return to ordinary reality with the soul parts held in my arms. As I sit up, I lean over and blow the soul parts into my client, first into the heart chakra and the remainder into the crown chakra. I can always feel the energy first in my arms and then as it moves into my client. I seal their aura with my hands or with a rattle and let them know the work is complete. I like to give my client some time to sit with the experience before I talk with them about it. If I am working from a distance, I do this part from within shamanic reality.

After they've had some time to be with the experience, I share the details of my journey with my client. I urge them to spend some time talking to their soul parts that have returned, asking whether they have information to share about why they left, what gifts they bring back, and how my client can make it comfortable for those soul parts to stay. Of course, for the last question, negotiation may be required, since a three-year-old soul part may want things that are impractical as for an adult. One example would be that if a young soul part wants ice cream and you are now lactose intolerant, you could remember what it was like to eat ice cream instead of actually eating it and making yourself sick. It's important to welcome those parts back and celebrate their return.

Following a soul retrieval, a client often continues to experience spontaneous soul return of soul parts coming back on their own, now that the process has been activated. This is part of why most people only need one soul retrieval, rather than ongoing sessions. Of course, soul return can also occur without any direct shamanic intervention. Many therapy techniques that have people getting in touch with their inner child could result in a soul return of that part. Energy healing can also cause a soul part to return naturally.

Some people experience soul retrieval as life changing; other people feel a subtler impact. We all experience soul loss as humans, but for some the losses are smaller and have less of an influence. I always encourage my clients to trust their intuition. The most powerful experiences happen when my client has a strong inner knowledge that they need a soul retrieval. However, if you feel inclined to explore a soul retrieval but don't feel a passionate need, you can still benefit.

For people who understand the concept of soul loss, whether or not they move forward with a soul retrieval, there is an opportunity to move through the world with much healthier energetic boundaries. It is good to become conscious of not giving away your soul parts, no matter how deeply you love someone. You can also set your intent to release any soul parts that you may have collected from others. When you release those parts, you free yourself of the burden of unusable energy. You also improve your energetic relationship to the people whose soul parts you have and place yourself more fully in right relationship with the universe. You don't need any shamanic training to release soul parts that belong to others. Just state your intent that any soul parts you have be returned to the people they belong to. You can ask your guides to help. If you want to, you can do a specific shamanic journey to release others' soul parts.

One of the questions I get asked very often is whether people can do soul retrieval journeys for themselves. This works very well for reclaiming soul parts that have been disowned or become separated through trauma. It's an advanced journey, so you'll want to make sure you feel very comfortable with the journey process first. In this case, set your intent and ask your guides for help and instruction.

However, when soul parts are with another person, having someone else do the journey to retrieve them is generally a better choice. I am a strong supporter of people empowering themselves and using shamanism as a tool for self-healing. But in this case, it's complex enough so that seeking the help of an experienced shamanic practitioner is a good idea.

I don't recommend you undertake to do this work for others without a great deal of practice and training in shamanic journeying and energy movement skills. In addition to the need for clear and accurate journey work, the transfer of the other person's energetic essence from nonordinary reality to ordinary reality and then into their physical body is not easy. Mishandling someone's soul parts accidentally could do them harm. Journeying for someone to discover their power animal or to get information for them is a much better bet when you're starting out.

PART 4
JOURNEYS, STORIES, EXPERIENCES

CHAPTER 12—JOURNEYS, STORIES, AND EXPERIENCES

In this section, I'd like to share some of my journeys that have not found their way into the text in other places.

It's important to understand that in shamanic reality, ten people could ask the same question and get twelve different answers. One of the most powerful aspects of shamanic reality is that it offers the chance to receive spiritual wisdom that is custom tailored for us—our guides recommend practices and lessons and convey information based on who we are individually. So please understand that when I share a journey, it is about what's true for me, not about what's objectively true.

Journey to beyond the moment of my own death

I took a class entitled "Shamanism, Dying, and Beyond" that included shamanic techniques for helping souls to cross over and move on. One of the journeys we did was to the moment beyond our own death, to investigate what is on the other side. Everyone had completely different experiences.

In shamanic reality, when someone is getting ready to die or to make a great change in their life, I often see them standing on a cliff, getting ready to go over. My guides showed me that the way to venture past the point of my own death in shamanic reality was to go over a cliff into a beautiful pink, orange, and gold mist. Taking a deep breath, I went over the cliff and into the mist.

On the other side, there was a big party going on where I was greeted by a number of people. Most of the deaths in my life have been of animals, and they were all there to greet me—dogs and cats and goats and a horse that had been my closest connections as a child and a teenager. There was a sense of celebration and reunion. After I had spent some time with them, I met with a council of people who seemed to be there to help me review my life. They were not judging or particularly serious and seemed to find the journey I was taking amusing but useful. We talked a little and I made some suggestions for what my next life might be like, but we agreed that it was way early to start talking about that.

I went on to start investigating the place. They showed me an area where people who choose to process pain or wounds could have a space to do this, as long as they chose. They also showed me an area where people could simply drop off old energy—pain, wounds, and so on. They would lift their baggage (in the form of suitcases) into a machine that transformed the energy into rainbows, putting that stagnant energy back into motion to be used for the good of everyone. I saw an area where people could pick up soul parts that had become separated or aspects of themselves that they had chosen not to take with them in order to have a certain life experience. I got the sense that there was as much time as anyone wished to rest and replenish, to visit with loved ones, and to think about the life that was finished. The journey was wonderful, but it was very clear to me and to those around me that I am currently very connected to my life.

Journey with the animals in my life

Taz

I live with a beautiful calico cat named Tazendra or Taz for short. Taz is a wise old soul with grandmother energy. She is completely clear about who she is. She and I are both willful beings and on the occasions when that comes up between us, the argument seems to be about which of us is the older soul. She loves me but she is also willing to sit back and watch me figure out my own path. She watched me learn shamanic journeying and energy healing and made it clear that she knew about this stuff before I figured it out.

On one occasion, I was doing a soul retrieval for a friend at my home. Shortly after I started my shamanic journey, Taz jumped up on my lap and lay down. Usually she leaves me alone when I'm journeying and I spent a moment wondering if I should push her down so I wouldn't be distracted. But she appeared in shamanic reality with me and let me know that she knew I was doing a soul retrieval and she had a reason for coming along. Of course, she didn't tell me what that reason was, but I got the sense of an older, wiser teacher saying to a student, "You're doing just fine, carry on." She held perfectly still for the rest of the journey and I promptly forgot she was there.

When I got to the final soul part I was to bring back, it was a three-year-old child curled up in a ball. The soul loss had occurred as the result of molestation and the child was crying. Her ability to trust and connect had been damaged so much that I couldn't reach her. At that point Taz walked over and began licking the tears off the child's face. The little girl threw her arms around Taz and held her tightly. Taz seemed to tell her that I was safe and okay, after which the little girl agreed to come with me.

When I told my friend, she told me about her favorite picture of herself at three with a calico cat that looked very much like Taz. That cat was very dear to her child self and my own wise calico knew that she would be needed when I began the work.

Morrigan

My other cat, Morrigan, is very different from the self-confident Taz. Morrigan is far and away the sweeter of the two, but there is a fragility to her. She doesn't like it when I enter shamanic reality—she can feel exactly when I leave and often cries and meows until I come back. She sometimes wakes me from a deep sleep if she feels I am wandering too far in my dreams. So I decided to use shamanic journeying in an effort to understand Morrigan.

My guides showed me that in a past life, she was my grandson, a sensitive, gentle soul with the ability to look between worlds. I was the only person who understood this boy and we lived in a world that valued practical, tough, no-nonsense men even more than we do today. While I lived, I insisted that the family honor him as he was, but when I died, he lost the only person who understood him and his protector. The family didn't understand the depth of the loss nor who he was as a person.

So Morrigan, who is in my life today as my cat, gets upset when I go away and tends to be clingy. The best compromise I have come up with for shamanic journeying is that when I journey and she starts to cry, I invite her to join me in shamanic reality. As soon as she shows up in the shamanic world, she stops crying. She generally joins me in shamanic reality looking about the size of an elephant. I believe she feels like I don't notice her as much as I should and so she's making sure there's no way I can miss her.

A goat

When I was growing up on a farm in northern California, one of my baby goats was bitten in the head by a rattlesnake. When I found her, her head was swollen to twice its normal size. We called the vet out and I spent hours holding her in my arms, completely focused on her. At the time, I had no idea of healing energy; I was merely amazed that I could sit so still, for so long, holding her and focusing on her, without becoming bored or restless.

By the end of the day, she was much better and I put her back out into the pasture. I went off to school the next morning and when I came home, instead of rushing out to check on her, I watched TV and hung out, so it was hours after I got home before I went out and found her dying. I gave her water and held her in my arms for the next hour until she died. Then I held her body and wept more intensely than I had in years. I was consumed with guilt and remorse, feeling that she had died because I had been selfish and failed to take care of her as I should.

When I took the shamanic class on death and dying, she came to me in a shamanic journey and gave me some additional information. She told me that she was meant to die at that time and nothing that I did or didn't do would have changed that outcome. Yes, if I'd come sooner I could have eased her passing a bit more, but the important gift I gave her was the chance to die in my arms. Her gift to me was the chance to truly cry. By that time I had built up this intense wall around my emotions and I simply never cried. When I wept over her death, it was a chance to release a great deal of pain that I had been keeping utterly suppressed. The experience touched me deeply and allowed me to release the guilt that I still carried regarding her death.

My soul retrieval

I first heard about soul retrieval in a class with Hank Wesselman. From the moment he mentioned it, I knew it was something I want to do and that I wanted to do with my mother. When I asked my mother, she agreed. I then contacted Jill Kuykendall, Hank's wife, and arranged for an appointment a few months later, her earliest opening. Jill emailed me a few questions about why I wanted a soul retrieval, what I wanted to heal, and so forth, and I wrote back describing some of the things from my childhood that I felt had resulted in soul loss. I spoke candidly about my inability to trust myself and my feelings about my family and my parents. When Jill wrote back via email, she included all the logistical details, when and where to show up, and I blithely forwarded the email to my father so he could print it out for my mother, not realizing that all the things I had written to Jill were included in that email.

A few weeks later my mother called and commented on my comments. I was horrified—I would certainly never risk hurting my parents with the unvarnished truth. I might communicate that information, but I wanted to phrase it gently, carefully, in such a way as not to hurt. My mother came very close to backing out of the soul retrieval but in the end decided to come with me. It was a turning point in our relationship.

The soul retrieval itself was beautiful—Jill spent hours with us, giving us the details of what to expect, how she did the work, and how to move forward after our soul retrieval. Because my mother and I went together, Jill did healing work for the maternal line as well as the soul retrieval itself. When I left I felt that I was filled absolutely to the brim with my own light and life energy. I had just been given the most beautiful, perfect gift ever, and, what's more, it was always intended to be mine. Missing childhood memories feel into place as if they'd never been missing and, overnight, I developed a deep and abiding sense of trust in myself. I also knew at that moment that much as I loved energy healing, if I only got one session with a client, a soul retrieval was what I'd want to give them, because it was so powerful.

Healing for others

One of the most enjoyable aspects of the work I do is getting to do healing journeys for other people. The spirits are so creative when it comes to shifting things.

One client asked for some help resetting the energy of her house. My guides showed me that part of the problem was that my client's husband's former wife was unconsciously sending a great deal of obsessive energy toward the house that she had once lived in. My guides showed me a way not to interfere with the ex-wife while protecting my client's home from that energy. They showed me that the home existed in shamanic reality in the current time as well as in the time when the ex-wife had lived there, sort of overlapping. They had me pick up and move the house from before over to the side. This way, the location that the energy flowed to from the ex-wife's obsession was no longer the same location as my client's current home.

Many of my clients have experienced sexual trauma as children. My guides show me how these patterns go back generation after generation, as the victim becomes the perpetrator. What they show me is that this energy of sexual abuse has been part of the way the people have explored the nature of power, taking turns being the one to misuse it and being the victim of its misuses. At this time, many old souls have taken on the experience of this trauma, not because they need to understand not to misuse sexuality, but in order to free the world from sexual abuses. Every time someone heals from sexual trauma, it becomes easier for others with similar trauma to heal. This healing is contributing to a universal consciousness and collective knowledge of how to release and heal sexual trauma so that it can stop being part of our world.

A stalker was troubling a friend of mine. I offered to do some shamanic work and my guides helped me cut away the energetic cords this person was sending to my friend. They allowed me to set up a mirror so that the energy sent toward my friend would be reflected away. They also helped me to strengthen her natural shielding and a couple of new power animals came in to provide additional protection.

I had a mother and daughter come to me for a soul retrieval together. In this case, there were some family themes of abuse and disconnection. My guides took me back to the first incident. In this case, the husband was physically abusive toward his wife. This was many generations ago when women had few options for supporting themselves on their own. It would have been hard for her to leave and harder still to support the child she was carrying. Because she was trapped in an abusive situation, this woman felt a great deal of ambivalence about her unborn child. While she loved it, she also resented it because it bound her more tightly to the situation. This situation—the domestic violence, the resentment, the sense of being trapped—created a complex energetic structure that got handed down through the generations. My guides showed me that this structure worked like a complex molecule, joining the family with other families with similar themes. My guides helped me offer healing and protection to the woman and dissolve the energetic structure that this created.

Another of my clients had had an abortion many years previously and asked me to do a journey to see if the soul needed help or healing. I went and found the soul that would have become the child. He told me that he had never meant to incarnate. Being conceived and then experiencing the abortion was absolutely perfect because it gave him the chance to have the smallest taste of being confined to a physical body without having to go through a full incarnation. In fact, he wanted my help. My client had actually sent a soul part of herself to be with him when she had the abortion. He was being held onto by this soul part and couldn't make it let go. So I talked to the soul part and explained that many years had passed and she had grown children of her own. She let go of the spirit of the boy and came back to my client.

IN CONCLUSION

I could write an entire book about the hundreds of journeys I have taken, across space and time, learning and experiencing everything from the mystical to the pragmatic. My guides have given me information on what to eat and my spiritual purpose with equal attention and love. They offer their energy to teach me, support me, and guide me, unconditionally, even when I'm crabby and impatient. Over the years, my shamanic journeys have been one of the richest experiences in my life. They have given me a great deal to think about, touched my emotions to the core, and shifted my physical experience. I've found healing, information, wisdom, joy, support, protection, and fun in my shamanic experiences.

The greatest gift I can offer you is the tools to access that world for yourself. It is my fondest hope that you will find the process of journeying as powerful, empowering, and fun as it has been for me. There's nothing else in my experience that quite compares with being able to talk directly to the spirits who have chosen to guide, support, and protect you. It may not be something you learn instantly, but with practice it can enrich your life immeasurably. But whatever use you make of it, I want to thank you for reading my book.

BIBLIOGRAPHY/RECOMMENDED READING

Shamanic Journeying: A Beginner's Guide, Sandra Ingerman. Colorado: Sounds True, 2004.

This book covers the basics of shamanic journeying. Sandra Ingerman has also written *Soul Retrieval* and *Welcome Home*, which are excellent books related to soul loss and soul retrieval.

The Journey to the Sacred Garden: A Guide to Traveling in the Spiritual Realms, Hank Wesselman. USA: Hay House, 2003.

This book also covers the basics of shamanic journey. In addition, Hank Wesselman deals with how to explore and use your place of power to affect change in your life.

Shaman, Healer, Sage: How to Heal Yourself and Others with the Energy Medicine of the Americas, Alberto Villoldo. New York: Harmony Books, 2000.

This book has good information about right alignment and right relationship to the universe.

The Way of the Shaman, Michael Harner. New York: HarperCollins, 1990.

This book is very much a part of the shamanic tradition for a modern, technological audience. However, I don't recommend it to beginners because the approach isn't as gentle as some of the later books.

The Dark Side of Light Chasers, Debbie Ford. New York: Riverhead Books, 1998.

This is the best book I've come across dealing with shadow work

Psychic Protection, Ted Andrews. USA: Dragonhawk Publishing, 1998.

Ted Andrews is one of my favorite authors. His writing is clear, accessible, and filled with compassion. I recommend this book for anyone who is feeling nervous about the unseen world or who is looking for ways to better manage the energy they take in from the world around them.

Spiritual Psychology—The Twelve Primary Life Lessons, Steve Rother. USA: Lightworker, 2004.

Steve Rother is a wonderful channel. I highly recommend his writing as well as his seminars and work. Check out www.lightworker.com for more information.

All Love: A Guidebook For Healing With Sekhem-Seichim-Reiki and SKHM, Diane Shewmaker. Washington: Celestial Wellspring Publications, 2000.

Diane Shewmaker's book is beautiful and contains excellent information about energy healing.

Prayers and Meditations of the Quero Apache, Maria Yraceburu. USA: Bear & Company, 2004.

Maria offers beautiful stories and traditional Quero Apache practices.

HEALING PRACTITIONERS AND OTHER RESOURSES

In addition to my own services, I highly recommend the following practitioners.

Jennifer Dyer, my cover artist, New Moon Design, 619-255-8070, jennifer@new-moon-design.com

William H. Stoddard, my copy editor, whswhs@mindspring.com

Margi Duran, Accupuncture, herbs, Traditional Chinese and Integrative Medicine, healingqi@cox.net, 619-807-4737

Laura Lee, trauma release and massage, www.lauraleereleasework.com

Nicole Francis, Nikki Bodyworks, Transformational energetic and structural bodywork www.nikkibodyworks.net

Marc Biagi, TarotScape, gifted psychic and tarot teacher, www.tarotscape.com

Nicole McVey, Tarot Reader,Reiki/Shamanic Healing, mcnik2@yahoo.com

Brenda Greystone, Energetic healing massage, bgraystone@email.com

Connie Russert, Tools for Transformation, gifted channel, seminar leader, author, www.toolsfortransformation.com

Jennifer "Tashiawna" Vause, Enlightened Energies, Awakening Divine Rememberance, Clearing, Reiki, 619-322-8050 tashiawna@yahoo.com

Yabyummy, Kypris and Steven Jay, Teaching Tantric Play, www.yabyummy.com, 760-522-2554

Kaliani, Cynthia Hupper, Reiki Master, Kundalini/Hatha Yoga, www.SoaringSpiritYoga.com

The Foundation for Shamanic Studies, Michael Harner's site on shamanism, www.shamanism.org

ACKNOWLEDGMENTS

Shortly after I began writing, it became clear to me that while I write extremely well compared to your average engineer, I don't write nearly as well as your average professional writer. So I would like to thank the people who helped me with writing critiques and edits: William H. Stoddard, Laura Kate Barrett, and Deborah Luria. The overall quality of my writing has been greatly improved by their assistance.

I also thank the people who had the greatest impact on my personal healing and growth prior to writing this book. More people have touched my life than I can possibly name, but those with the largest impact include Arne Liss, Evan Thomas, Michael Hartzel, Deborah Luria, Laura Kate Barrett, Serena and Phil Poisson, Steve and Barbara Rother, Carol Holaday, Jill Kuykendall, and Diane Shewmaker. This book includes much of their wisdom. And I would like to thank some of my best cheerleaders for their support: Ryan Latimer, Dominique Colbert, my Temple Priestess sisters, once more, Ms. Laura Kate Barrett, my mother, and Jesse Duran.

Thank you to Jennifer Dyer for the lovely cover art.

Finally, my expressions of gratitude would be incomplete without talking about my spirit guides. They think it's very funny that I feel the need to formally acknowledge them in this way. Yet they have always been there for me, through the darkest times as well as the most joyful. Their support has been unconditional and always available. This book would not exist without them.

About the Author

Katie Weatherup is a shamanic practitioner, a Reiki master, and a mechanical engineer. Her unique perspective on shamanism centers on the application of each person's spiritual and intuitive abilities to the issues attending everyday life from a pragmatic, "what works" point of view. She helps people find their way back to themselves, all the parts they have lost, forgotten, denied, and disowned.

Shamanism is a staple of her healing business, Hands over Heart. Currently residing in San Diego, she teaches classes in shamanic journeying and offers individual healing sessions and soul retrieval. Katie's commitment to healing work is part of her deep commitment to her own growth and healing. For more information, visit her website at www.handsoverheart.com.

Breinigsville, PA USA
16 June 2010
239977BV00003B/118/A